A DEAR AND NOBLE BOY

THE LIFE AND LETTERS OF LOUIS STOKES 1897–1916

Edited by

R.A. BARLOW AND H.V. BOWEN

LEO COOPER

LONDON

First published in Great Britain in 1995 by
LEO COOPER
190 Shaftesbury Avenue, London WC2H 8JL
an imprint of
Pen & Sword Books Ltd,
47 Church Street,
Barnsley, South Yorkshire S70 2AS

A CIP record for this book is available from the British Library

ISBN 0 85052 425 3

Typeset by CentraCet Limited, Cambridge
Printed in England by
Redwood Books Ltd.
Trowbridge, Wilts.

CONTENTS

ACKNOWLEDGEMENTS

We are grateful to the Governing Body of Rugby School for allowing us access to the School Archive, and to the Archivist, Jenny Macrory, for her most helpful and patient advice and criticism over a number of years. Our task was made much easier by the fact that Mr J.D. Pickles of the Cambridge Antiquarian Society did a great deal of important preliminary work on the Stokes papers before they were passed on to Rugby School. David Ray kindly allowed us to make use of his unrivalled detailed knowledge of the Old Rugbeians who died during the First World War. We would also like to thank Mr M. Little of the Royal Marines Museum, Southsea, for help in providing background material on the history of the Royal Marines Light Infantry. Above all, of course, thanks must go to our families for their patience, good humour, and encouragement: they should see us a bit more often now that our regular editorial conferences have come to an end!

EDITORIAL NOTE

Unless otherwise stated, the primary source materials used in this book are to be found in the Archive Room at Rugby School. We have been able to date with some degree of accuracy most of the Stokes letters through postmarks on envelopes or by reference to internal evidence, but where this has not been possible we have placed them in their most likely position in the chronological order within the collection. During the transcription process we have, in the interests of consistency, modernized spelling and punctuation in the very few cases where this was necessary.

We have managed to identify the vast majority of the individuals referred to in the letters, and we have supplied biographical information in the form of a footnote at the time of their first mention in the text. In order to be concise, we have supplied only brief details of school careers and war service; we have not gone further and added information about post-war activities for this would have added great length to the notes. In the case of Rugbeians, we have referred to their years in school and to the house to which they belonged. Because in most cases houses used to take the name of the housemaster, and would change them at the time of a new appointment, we have followed common practice and given the name of a house as it was when a boy first entered the school. Unless otherwise stated, biographical information was derived from the following printed sources: A.T. Michell (ed.), *Rugby School Register*, vol.iii: May 1874–May 1904 (Rugby, 1904); G. Higginbotham (ed.), *Rugby School Register*, vol.iv: January 1892–September 1921 (Rugby, 1929); *Memorials of Rugbeians who Fell in the Great War* (7 vols., privately printed by the Medici Society, no date). Throughout the book we have used the abbreviation SH for School House and OR for Old Rugbeian. In general, the place of publication of works cited is London, unless otherwise stated.

INTRODUCTION

HOME AND FAMILY

1897–1911

Thousands of young British men made the very rapid transition from school to front line during the First World War, and many of them died within a few months of abandoning their books for the last time. One such boy was Louis Stokes who died at Beaumont Hamel on the Somme in November, 1916, less than a year after leaving Rugby School. He was not a military hero, but an ordinary junior officer who met an early and inglorious end in no-man's-land during his first close-quarter encounter with the enemy. In that sense he was no different from thousands of his contemporaries who died shortly after going over the top into action. But what marks out Louis Stokes for special attention is the fact that he left behind him a rich chronicle and detailed account of his teenage years in the form of hundreds of letters he wrote to his family. These letters furnish us with an account of Louis' life which covers his time at Rugby betwen 1911 and 1915; they provide a lengthy and reasoned explanation of his decision to join the armed forces; and they offer a full description of his brief career in the Royal Marines Light Infantry.

Of course, many well-known, first-hand individual accounts of the First World War have found their way into print, but few, if any, can offer such a penetrating insight into the life of one of those who trod the well-worn path from public school to Western Front. For it is the complete, all-embracing nature of Louis Stokes' letters which make them unique. Not only does he provide us with a colourful and intelligent account of his time at Rugby and in the armed forces, but, such was his sharp eye for detail and his ability to recount episodes from daily life in the form of entertaining and telling anecdotes, that he also provides us with the means to identify and understand some of the forces and influences that shaped the mind, outlook and assumptions of a public schoolboy on the eve of the Great War. This alone would make the letters a valuable source for those interested in military and social history, but in addition Louis explained at some length his emotional response to the tumultuous events of 1914–16. He was obliged to do this because his father, a clergyman, was a committed and active pacifist who opposed his decision to join the school's Officer Training Corps in 1914. Louis was forced to justify his reasons for responding to the call to arms and, during the course of a lengthy debate with his father, much is revealed about the motives and values of one of the millions who was swept along on the tide of patriotic fervour that characterized the early years of the War.

From the time Louis Stokes was thirteen his father kept every scrap of paper related to his life and activities. Thus not only do the Stokes papers contain letters written from school and war, but they also include reports, notebooks, poems, essays, bills, receipts and photographs. Moreover, memorials and tributes written by friends, officers and teachers after his death help to provide us with as complete a picture as possible of his life. There are, nevertheless, some limitations that must be borne in mind when reading this material. Memorials are often of limited value to the historian for they always, and not surprisingly, accentuate the positive side of an individual's character and achievements. Tributes written by officers on active service to grieving parents are not designed to paint an accurate picture of the circumstances surrounding an individual's death. Thus the noble spirit of sacrifice is emphasized, while the grim realities of trench warfare are often translated into formulaic references to a well-liked character meeting a sudden, untimely end involving no pain and suffering. More importantly, perhaps, the correspondence upon which this book is based is very one-sided, because Louis, like most boys of his age, did not keep and preserve the many letters that were written to him. This is, of course, frustrating at times because the voice of a key figure such as Louis' father is seldom heard, and only one side of an argument or dispute can be advanced. Nevertheless, this state of affairs does have its compensations, for it allows a continuous narrative to be developed as one follows without interruption the news transmitted by Louis to the family home in Cambridge. As with all such letters, there is some material that is mundane, inconsequential and repetitive, but for the most part episodes and events are described with vigour, humour and no little style.

Indeed, at times it is necessary to remind oneself that one is reading the work of a thirteen- or fourteen-year-old boy, such is the sustained quality of the prose.

The figure that looms largest in Louis' correspondence is his father, the Reverend Henry Stokes, because, although the weekly letter home was always addressed to the whole family or to 'Mother and Dad', it is quite clear that Louis wrote with his father in mind. Thus, while occasional asides are made to his mother about the state of his health, or the need not to worry about the rigours of Rugby football, the contents were largely determined by what his father wanted to hear. Accordingly, accounts of sermons feature prominently, and, despite Louis' occasional protestation, he often provided a blow-by-blow, word-by-word account of lengthy orations in the school Chapel. Similarly, Louis was eager to provide his father with news of his scholarly endeavours, so almost every letter written during his time at school contains some report of progress or the lack of it. Yet, fortunately, Louis does not appear to have felt unduly constrained by the need to please his father, and he also reported a full range of news on a wide variety of themes. Reports of football and cricket matches sit alongside well-observed sketches of incidents in everyday life, and, while during his time at Rugby the focus remained on school and house, comments were also made on matters of current national interest such as the miners' strike of 1912, the development of the health service and, of course, the progress of the War.

After Louis' death in 1916, his letters, papers and effects were kept together, first by his father, and then by his youngest sister, Amy Stokes, the last surviving member of the family. When she died in the 1980s the papers, now stored in a magnificent battered suitcase, were deposited with the Cambridge Antiquarian Society. The Society's Honorary Librarian, Mr J.D. Pickles, then did much valuable work by sorting, arranging and classifying the papers, and he eventually took the decision to pass the material on to Rugby School. The collection is now housed in the Archive Room in the School Museum, and the wheel has come full circle, for Louis' letters now have a permanent home a hundred yards away from School House where many of them were first written.

Louis Mander Stokes was born in Cambridge on 19 July, 1897. One of four children, he was the only son of the Reverend Henry Paine Stokes and Sophie Emmeline Stokes, *née* Mander. His father had been born in Margate in 1849, the second son of the Reverend John Stokes and Mary Stokes, *née* Kinton.[1] Mary Stokes was soon left as a relatively young widow with five sons, and Henry was educated at the Orphan School in Slough before going up to Cambridge. Henry seems to have become something of a father-figure to his youngest brother Louis, paying for him to be put through college, and he was grief-stricken when Louis died at the age of thirty-four. In later years Henry Stokes often spoke to his own children about 'Uncle Louis' and there can be little doubt that he hoped his own son would follow in the academic footsteps of his dead brother.[2] Little is known about Louis' mother, apart from the fact that she was the daughter of C.B. Mander of Wolverhampton. She first met Henry Stokes when he was serving as Vicar of St Peter's, Wolverhampton, and the couple married in 1895 when she was thirty-nine years of age. The Stokes family settled in Cambridge shortly afterwards, when Henry was appointed as Vicar of St Paul's, whose parish church and vicarage lie close to Fenner's cricket ground, half-way between the city centre and the railway station. This move marked a return to familiar territory for the Vicar, for he had previously been a student at Corpus Christi College during the 1870s before clerical service took him away to Berkshire, Bristol and Wolverhampton. By picking up the threads of his scholarly career, Henry Stokes became a well-known figure in Cambridge academic and literary circles, and between 1909 and 1911 he served as President of the local antiquarian society. He was the author of a large number of books and pamphlets on a wide range of subjects. Originally a Shakespearean scholar, in later years he wrote extensively on the history and topography of Cambridge, and his services to Jewish history were recognized in 1914 when he became President of the Jewish Historical Society. A doctoral thesis on the laws of gambling was completed in 1897, prompting one obituarist to remark rather drily that 'of gambling itself he must have had small or no practical experience'. In 1912 he became an Honorary Fellow of his old college. His scholarly legacy was quite a considerable one and his works are still cited today, but nothing better represents the general tone of Henry Stokes' career as an antiquarian and historian than the fact that following his death his personal archive was found to contain notes on all kinds of subjects scribbled on thousands and thousands of slips of paper.[3]

By the time Louis left home to go to Rugby in 1911 his father had become something of a local character, not least because of his striking physical appearance. As photographs of him testify, he was a large, formidable-looking figure, yet appearances were deceptive and a memorial of her father written by Amy Stokes in the 1960s or 1970s paints a loving portrait of Henry Stokes as a sensitive and devoted family man.[4] For while Louis grew up in an environment where scholarship, study and serious conversation were part-and-parcel of everyday life, it is clear that Henry was not a stereotypical dry-as-dust antiquarian who was entirely out of touch with contemporary society and popular pastimes. He might have considered the New Testament as appropriate reading for a family holiday by the sea, but at the same time he imparted a passion for cricket into his son, and the two were regular attenders together at Fenner's during the holidays, and even in his eightieth year Henry Stokes made his annual pilgrimage to Lord's for the Varsity match. Moreover, in the context of modern politics and world affairs, it is clear that Louis' father was a man committed to deeply held minority views. He was profoundly offended by, and bitterly opposed to, the War, finding the conflict both senseless and immoral, and it is not surprising to find him described by one obituarist as a 'staunch liberal of the Gladstone school'. Equally, it is not surprising to find evidence in Louis' letters that he became actively involved in campaigns to promote the cause of conciliation and arbitration between the warring nations. The news of Louis' death hit his father very hard indeed, and, according to Amy Stokes, despite outward appearances he never fully recovered. The family moved from St Paul's vicarage in 1917, when Henry Stokes became Rector of Little Wilbraham. In his later years (by now Honorary Canon of Ely) he devoted considerable energy to his studies, and he continued to publish work up until the time of his death at the age of eighty-two in 1931.

After leaving St Faith's Preparatory School in Cambridge, Louis entered Rugby School in September, 1911. The choice of school seems to have been dictated in part by the fact that his uncle, J.H. Mander, had been at the school between 1882 and 1888. Moreover, although the numbers of sons of the clergy at the school had been steadily diminishing for some time, Rugby had always had a strong tradition of recruiting boys from clerical backgrounds.[5] Although Louis was not successful in his attempt to win a scholarship, he seems to have impressed the headmaster enough to have had his name added to Dr A.A. David's 'list' of entrants to his boarding house, School House. This preferential treatment might have been sufficient to persuade Henry that his son would be in good hands if he went to Rugby, and it might have been reassuring for him to know that Louis would find himself in the company of many boys from similar upper-middle class backgrounds. For while some parents of pupils at Rugby came from old aristocratic and gentry families, an ever-increasing proportion belonged to the business, commercial and professional classes, and, not least because of its geographical location, Rugby attracted a far higher proportion of its pupils from the North and Midlands than did the other major public schools. But whatever lay behind the choice of Rugby, there is no evidence that education for Louis at any other school was ever contemplated.

In his first term at Rugby, Louis went, as tradition demanded, to one of the smaller 'waiting' boarding houses, Lawrence Sheriff House run by the Reverend Llewellyn Bullock.[6] Then, during the course of Louis' first term, it was confirmed that in January, 1912, he would transfer to School House. This meant that for most of his school career he found himself living at the very heart of Rugby's community, for not only was School House located at the centre of the school's site adjacent to the Close, but it was the oldest of the boarding houses. Moreover, the status and prestige of School House was reinforced by the fact that, in keeping with tradition, the headmaster, the 'Bidge', not only lived with his family on the 'private side' of the house, but he also acted as housemaster to the eighty or so boys who lived there. This meant that, unlike some of their contemporaries who regarded the headmaster as a rather dim and distant figure, School House boys saw a great deal of the man who not only ran the school but who also acted *in loco parentis* for them. Thus, in Louis' letters the figure of Dr David looms very large indeed. Not only did Louis dutifully record for his father the sentiments expressed in David's many sermons, but his notes on conversations and meetings reveal much about the ideas, methods and principles of the man who guided the school through a difficult period in its history. Moreover, the letters trace the growth and development of the relationship between master and pupil. David undoubtedly found Louis to be a difficult, complex and challenging boy, yet he also perceived him to be a pupil of great talent and potential. Louis, for his part, despite his protestations about the length of his headmaster's sermons, respected David, was fiercely loyal towards him at times and turned to him as something akin to a father figure for advice, guidance and support, particularly during the war years. The relationship between the two is one of central importance in this book, because, directly and indirectly, David exercised great influence over Louis, and the headmaster's attitudes and ideas shaped, to a considerable degree, the outlook and development of his young pupil.

Many aspects of life at Rugby were harsh. The daily routine, including a lesson before breakfast, could be a demanding one; there was a lack of privacy; the living accommodation was spartan; the diet was fairly basic; and illness, disease, injury and even death all formed part of school life. Such conditions, not to mention the competitive nature of all aspects of the system, could make boys unhappy and homesick, as was the case with Louis' contemporary who fled from the school in February, 1912.[7] Yet, on the whole, Rugbeians seem to have put a brave face on things, for it was considered a virtue to display manliness and unsentimentality in public. Louis, despite the occasional expression of regret, seems to have been quite content during his time at the school. There were few complaints in his letters home, and at times he displayed great enthusiasm for games and life in School House. He constantly referred to his existence as being 'ripping', and on the whole he seems to have enjoyed a relatively carefree existence.

Yet it would be wrong to characterize Louis as a typical product of the public-school system. His background meant that he could never be that, but, more importantly, the complex nature of his character set him aside from many of his contemporaries, and in some ways he possessed very special talents. Like all teenagers, he tended to see the world in black and white terms; that is, he either liked someone or he didn't, and thus many of his pen-portraits of masters are distinctly unflattering at times. All too often, people were arrogantly dismissed as being stupid or foolish, and few of those characters were perceived as having any redeeming qualities. Once his mind was made up about someone, he was not prepared or able to change it, the only notable exception being his attitude towards his tutor, J.H.B. Lockhart.[8] This began as something akin to hero worship, but deteriorated steadily thereafter for reasons that are not altogether clear. Stubborness was a characteristic commented on by a number of people who knew Louis well, and in the eyes of the authorities he came to be regarded as someone who could at times be difficult, obstinate and lacking in motivation. A semi-permanent scowl probably didn't help his cause. Yet in spite of these adolescent shortcomings, some, most notably the headmaster, recognized that beneath the surface lay considerable academic potential. For while Louis' reports often comment on a lack of motivation or 'slackness', there were glimpses of real quality in some of the pieces of work he produced. Nowhere was this more the case than in the field of composition where Louis' talents were given full rein to good effect. Several times his work was referred to David for the ultimate Rugby accolade, a Copy, and the headmaster later paid his former pupil the considerable retrospective tribute of publishing (anonymously) two of his pieces of work as being representative of the very best produced during his time at Rugby. Alongside 'R. L. Stevenson' and 'Fires', which Louis wrote in 1911 and 1912 respectively, David stated quite simply that 'they cannot fairly be cited . . . as fruits of our teaching, for clearly this boy was already beyond it.'[9] No higher tribute could be paid to Louis than this, and all the qualities implied in David's testimony shine through in the letters that follow.

NOTES TO INTRODUCTION

1   This account of Louis' family is based on J.A. Venn (comp.), *Alumni Cantabrigiensis: A Biographical List of All Known Students, Graduates and Holders of Office at the University of Cambridge, From the Earliest Times to 1900*, Part II, 1752–1900, vol vi. (Cambridge, 1954), 51–2; and Amy Stokes, 'I Too Had a Father', a typed memoir, probably written in the 1960s, which is now kept in the Local Collection in Cambridge City Library.

2   Louis Stokes (b.1852), who entered Corpus Christi College, Cambridge in 1876, died in 1886.

3   W.M. Palmer, 'Report on the Papers of H.P. Stokes', *Proceedings of the Cambridge Antiquarian Society*, 33 (1933), 168.

4   Amy Stokes, 'I Too Had a Father.'

5   T.W. Bamford, *The Rise of the Public Schools* (1967), pp.42, 215.

6   A.T. Michell (ed.), *Rugby School Register*, vol.iii: May 1874–May 1904 (Rugby, 1904), p.iv. Bullock was on the staff between 1902 and 1925.

7   See below, pp.45. For a description of the unhappy early days of one boy in the school see Robert Collis, *The Silver Fleece: An Autobiography* (1936), pp.29–34.

8   John Harold Bruce Lockhart, who was appointed to the staff in 1912, later became headmaster of his old school, Sedbergh.

9   A.A. David, *Life and the Public Schools* (1932), p.91.

PART ONE

RUGBY SCHOOL,

September 1911–July 1914

In 1911 Rugby School was a community of 580 boys and thirty-two masters, and, like all major public schools, its organization and structure was based on the house system. The house system had, of course, been developed by Thomas Arnold during his time at Rugby and, although many modifications had been made by subsequent headmasters, Arnold's influence was still present in the general way each house was organized and governed eighty or so years later. Indeed, one master conceded in 1911 that at times Rugby was still 'Arnold-ridden' and that the system by which the school operated was very much 'Arnold's system, and is of the blood and bone and fibre of her constitution today.'[1] There were nine major boarding houses in 1911, in addition to the Town House for those who lived locally. For all boys, school life centred on the house: they ate and slept there; they worked in studies or 'dens' there; they formed friendships there; and they represented the house at games and sports. A boy's house was held to be superior to all others and this gave the occupants a sense of common identity that was often reinforced by distinctive house colours, badges, ties, traditions, rituals and ceremonies. This meant that loyalty to a house was of paramount importance to a boy, and much was made of house spirit and strength. Loosely superimposed over this house-based system were school rules and codes of behaviour which were enforced by the heads of houses, the Levée, but only rarely, as in the case of inter-school or 'foreign' games fixtures, were displays of school spirit and identity made public. In short, boys belonged to a house, while they were little more than members of the school at large.

Many of the features of house life were defined by the boys themselves, and hierarchies within the house were regulated and reinforced by dining-room seating plans, study allocation and fagging arrangements. The whole operation was run, nominally at least, by a housemaster and non-resident tutors who were members of the teaching staff, but considerable responsibility was given to prefects or 'sixths', an élite who were granted significant powers in matters of routine administration and discipline. In practice, this meant that the sixth had the authority to inflict punishment ranging from caning to lines on their fellow pupils, and masters did not interfere in such matters. Indeed, as one pupil who was at the school in the early 1900s later recalled, there was an unwritten law that 'no act or word on the part of a master must appear to question the authority of a sixth.'[2] Because of this, most masters chose not to venture onto the boys' territory in the boarding houses, and in one case, which was probably typical, it was reported that a housemaster 'did not pass beyond the dining hall into our part of the House more than twice in two years.'[3] Such a state of affairs ran the obvious risk of allowing boys to establish corrupt and brutal régimes, but on the whole, according to those who experienced life in the boarding houses, corporal punishment was not frequent, even though some sickening beatings, 'sixth lickings', were administered by heads of houses from time to time.[4] Most prefects appear to have taken their duties and responsibilities seriously, and while few of them could aspire to Arnold's ideal that they become the 'guardians of morality and protectors of the weak', they did, on the whole at least, wield their authority with moderation and good sense. This was thought by many to be the ideal sort of training for those who would in later life rise to the top of the professions, military, civil service and colonial administration.[5] Even observers with a broad sense of educational perspective were of the opinion that the sixth system within the houses was 'the core and essence of the school and of Rugby's distinctive contribution to education.'[6]

The academic structure and organization of the school was quite complex, with a large number of divisions, grades and labels serving to define the hierarchy. On the whole, though, the curriculum remained predominantly classical, with some progress being made towards the development and integration of the sciences, a state of affairs which reflected the fact that Rugby had long been ahead of its major competitors in its commitment to the teaching of science.[7] It was later reported that many of the parents attracted to Rugby at this time found that the education provided in the school was 'solid, sensible, and genuine', and one individual commended the headmaster for providing a type of learning 'with no nonsense about it'.[8] After studying a common set of subjects in his first year in a lower middle form, a boy moved into one of two blocks, classical or modern, in the upper middles.[9] The only real difference between the two blocks was that Greek continued to be studied on the classical side, while German replaced it on the modern side. Chemistry and physics were now studied by all boys. Most of the lessons were taught by form masters, and hence boys had up to twenty lessons a week under the supervision of one individual, while a system of sets, graded by ability, operated for the study of mathematics, German, and Greek. The basic division between classics and moderns continued into the upper school, but, while the classics became increasingly specialized with a view to preparing candidates for entry to Oxford or Cambridge, the moderns were still provided with a relatively broad-based general education. Two other 'sides' were introduced for senior boys. The 'specialists' followed courses in mathematics and science, while the army class prepared candidates for entry to Sandhurst or Woolwich.[10] Depending on which side he was on, a boy moved up through the fifth forms to the twenty and the sixth, with the academic élite of the school being formed by members of the lower and upper bench on the classical side, the latter of whom were taught by the headmaster, as tradition demanded.

While the general educational framework appears to have been quite narrow and rigid, there was an element of choice which meant that boys could move away, in part at least, from a straightforward classical syllabus. However, few concessions were made for those who were not academically competent, and boys did not necessarily move up through the school at a uniform pace in the company of colleagues of the same age. Life in the form room, or 'school' as it was known, was organized around a competitive system designed to maximize industry and effort, if not understanding. Weekly orders and the regular calculation of form positions provided masters with a crude guide towards pupils' progress and consistent achievement was rewarded with promotion to a higher form. Those who failed to perform adequately were obliged to 'stay down' while their friends moved up to higher forms, and they ran the risk of incurring a beating from their form master if their work was deemed to be unsatisfactory.[11] This general practice, which David later condemned and criticized at some length,[12] had developed from the system that had been in operation in the early years of the nineteenth century when the bulk of the school had been taught together in one large room, Big School, with boys moving around the room, up the hierarchy, from bench to bench, master to master, as they successfully completed each stage of their work with an oral test or 'construe'. Of course, such a system meant that some older boys were held back in junior forms, and they ran the risk of being 'superannuated' if they did not make progress after four terms, while bright, industrious individuals found themselves moving rapidly up the school towards the sixth. This state of academic affairs was then reflected in the way that positions of responsibility and influence were filled, and even though scholars were not allowed to enter the sixth until they were sixteen, it was not uncommon to find boys exercising authority over some who were older than themselves. Not surprisingly, as Louis' letters reveal, in some cases this practice met with hostility and derision in equal measure among those boys who were passed over by the authorities when jobs and offices were distributed.

The boys in the lower forms in the years immediately before the War were fortunate to have been taught by a small group of highly motivated, reform-minded masters headed by Roger Raven.[13] This group, taking a lead from the headmaster, devoted much thought to teaching practice and techniques. They adopted the 'direct' method of teaching French, and one of their number, J.H. Simpson, was of the opinion that in English lessons a 'real revolution' took place as boys were encouraged to develop the creative aspects of their work on subjects of their own choosing in place of the study of set classical texts.[14] Yet, while the agents of change might enthuse about their work, it is doubtful whether those on the receiving end noticed any great alteration in the ways in which they were being taught. Of course, the boys lacked any sense of long-term perspective which could allow them to make comparisons of technique and method, but Louis' letters point to an educational experience that was largely ordered on very traditional lines, both in terms of structure and content.[15] He certainly does not appear to have been particularly inspired by a great deal of what went on in the form room, yet it was not in a Rugbeian's nature to praise unduly either masters or academic work, and from time to time he was prompted into feverish bouts of academic activity and reading which were motivated by more than the nature of the competitive system, or the simple need to please his father. Perhaps the influence of the reformers was most effectively passed from master to pupil in an informal context, through conversation and friendship, rather than through the medium of structured form-room teaching. But, whatever the tangible effects of changes in teaching methods, J.H. Simpson, who was well qualified to speak of such matters, thought that boys at Rugby were as well taught as any in England at the time, so much so that it could be argued that no school 'turned out a finer product'. Yet he also identified serious limitations to the type of education on offer at Rugby. He doubted whether any real progress was being made with the teaching of ordinary and dull boys, and he recognized that outside the classroom 'their emotional education had been starved' to the point that senior boys were leaving the school not yet equipped with any basic philosophy of life.[16]

Beyond the house and form room, routine demanded regular attendance at Chapel. Religion loomed large in the life of every pupil, if only because daily worship provided one of the few occasions when the whole school met together. From the boys' point of view, Chapel represented a compulsory activity which had to be endured rather than actively supported, and consequently behaviour in services was reported as being very poor.[17] In part this was because services were invariably long and tedious, but perhaps as important was the fact that the religious instruction received by the boys was, on the whole, orthodox and uncritical. Only during the course of pre-confirmation classes could any form of religious controversy be engaged, as was the case with Louis in his meetings with his tutor, Lockhart. In the main, religion at Rugby bore little relevance to everyday life or to the wider community, even though it is noticeable that Dr David's sermons did focus on current affairs from time to time. Accordingly, critics were able to argue that Rugbeians were ill-prepared to meet with, and engage, the problems confronting Christianity in the modern world, and it seems that few pupils of the Edwardian period took up holy orders in later life.[18]

All pupils were obliged to take part in a wide variety of athletic activities on a regular basis. Football was played by all boys in the autumn and spring terms, while cricket dominated proceedings in the summer. Cross-country running (including the long-standing Crick Run) and the athletic sports were added to the programme just before Easter, and Rugby fives, shooting, swimming, boxing and rackets allowed boys to pursue individual minority interests. No one, though, could escape from team games which, to a large extent, were organized and refereed by the boys themselves. Competent senior players in cricket or football found themselves on 'Big Side', attempting to find a place in the school XI or XV, while other boys participated in games graded by levels of skill and ability. Bookish, scholarly boys could not escape from the cult of games, particularly in the lower and middle school, for not only was there a compulsory weekly session of 'Swedish gymnastics', but they were also obliged to take part in different forms of inter-house competition. Those who were deemed not even to be competent enough for selection in house teams gathered together as 'remnants' on a field some way from the school to produce a game between two sides, the form of which was described by one observer as a 'perambulating conversazione, varied by occasional spells of football'.[19] Another commentator, writing from bitter personal experience, pointed to the fact that in the summer boys were obliged to spend hours and hours playing 'ineffably boring' games of cricket, which they had no interest in, or aptitude for, whatsoever.[20] Escape from compulsory cricket must have been greeted with considerable relief by the more scholarly members of the sixth.

The emphasis remained heavily in favour of house-based sport, but a handful of inter-school fixtures was played each year, including football matches against Uppingham, Cheltenham and various Oxford Colleges, and cricket matches againt Uppingham, Clifton and Marlborough. These were important school occasions, but even they were overshadowed by the final of the house match competitions, 'cock house match'. It was said at the time, and Louis' letters bear testimony to this, that it was the ambition of every Rugbeian to play in a winning cock house team, and for a member of a house to fail to attend a house match as a spectator was, in the words of one master, 'to ask for trouble'.[21]

In view of Rugby's unique contribution to the development of games, it is not surprising to find that athletic ability was rewarded with prestige and status within the school community. In this sense Rugby was no different from any other major public school of the period. Even so, observers were quick to point out that the average standard of the players in team sports was fairly poor, and reform of the system was needed.[22] Lockhart, himself a Scottish football international in 1913, commented on this several times to Louis, and while he was undoubtedly making the point in a light-hearted and provocative manner, he did draw attention to the fact that games were organized in an unsatisfactory fashion. Moreover, there was very little coaching available to boys, and this meant that those who had little interest in games remained untutored in even the basics.[23] Yet, while this approach failed to produce many players of real quality, despite obvious exceptions such as R.W. Poulton and A.D. Stoop, it did have some beneficial consequences because the cult of games, while at times excessive, did not get entirely out of hand. Pupils were not promoted to positions of responsibility on the basis of athletic skill alone, for they had to display some evidence of intelligence and scholarly endeavour as well. At the same time, while Rugby had its fair share of badges, caps and colours awarded for athletic achievement, it managed to place them in their proper perspective, allowing one observer later to remark that 'games were never quite accorded the reverence which they commanded at too many schools of that time . . . the distinctive millinery worn by prominent games players [had been reduced], and the sixth system and the school's ingrained hatred of ostenta- tion saved Rugby from the worst absurdites of athleteocracy.'[24] Louis' letters could perhaps be cited as evidence to contradict this comment, for, like so many of his contemporaries, he remained preoccupied with games throughout his time at Rugby. However, he was a fit, healthy boy, a competent all-round athlete, and his family background gave him an interest in games of all sorts. Rugby allowed him to indulge his passion for sport, and, as the mood took him, he developed an active interest in football, cricket, athletics, fives, running and boxing, the last serving as a necessary antidote to the unsatisfactory nature of his confirmation service in the school Chapel.

The Officer Training Corps represented an important extension of outdoor activity. Rugby's links with the armed forces went back to the beginning of the nineteenth century when the school had been the first in the country to establish a volunteer brigade, but it had not been until 1860 that a cadet force had been established on a permanent footing. In 1908, as part of Haldane's plans to establish a territorial reserve force, the Rifle Volunteer Brigade was renamed as the Officer Training Corps, and it was this organization that was to provide so many boys with a stepping stone into the armed forces in 1914 and 1915. The OTC is examined in detail below (see pp.82–5), but suffice it to say at this stage that it seems fair to concur with J.H. Simpson's assessment that for all Rugby's outward display of military zeal, the school in 1914 was, like most other public schools, 'not in the least militaristic'.[25] As if to underline this point, at a debate held in the school in 1911 the motion 'that war is a curse to humanity' was carried by 168 votes to 100.[26]

Chapel, games and the Corps gave boys little time to pursue out-of-school activities, legal or otherwise, of their own. This of course was the intention behind such a programme of vigorous activity, but it meant that there was little time available for the development of minority interests or pursuits. There was a well-attended debating society; a popular natural history society devoted much time to a wide range of scientific activity outside the classroom; and small groups of the academic élite met weekly in one of two exclusive literary societies, Eranos and Anonymi. But on the whole most boys spent a great deal of their time in organized mass pursuits and this gave rise to the criticism from dissidents within the Common Room that Rugbeians were being forced into mindless, regimented activity that was affecting their ability to think for themselves. Louis reported in early 1914 that Roger Raven's attempt to establish a reading society foundered because of a lack of support among the boys, and this would have been grist to the mill of those who argued that Rugby was developing into an anti-intellectual establishment where scholarly activity was frowned upon by the pupils. Although the school had a long tradition of academic excellence and had produced literary and political figures of the first rank, it was felt by some that the balance had swung too far in favour of those who advocated the merits of outdoor activity, with the result that the development of a healthy intellectual environment was being stifled. It was concerns and frustrations such as these that prompted one master, Hubert Podmore,[27] himself an Old Rugbeian, to attempt to stir the Common Room out of its state of complacency by reading them a provocative paper entitled 'Why don't Rugbeians think?'[28]

Podmore's paper reflected the belief that boys were developing a narrow outlook, but of course it is impossible to say with any certainty what Rugbeians did think, because diverse opinions always find expression in any community of 500 individuals, even if the members of that community are drawn from a fairly limited range of backgrounds. Nevertheless, identifying majority prevailing opinion among the boys is aided by the survival in print of the records of the senior debating society. The views expressed in such societies are not necessarily representative of attitudes in the school at large, but the reports of proceedings in the school magazine, the *Meteor*, are broadly suggestive. Between 1910 and 1914 the society voted against women's suffrage, it disapproved of the existence of the Labour Party and it supported unionist resistance to the Home Rule Bill. These results, all with large majorities, point to a broadly Conservative outlook within the School, yet the decision on women's suffrage was later reversed, and in 1910, on separate occasions, the society both approved and disapproved of the formation of another Liberal government. On matters closer to home, the society declared that public-school education was not antiquated and that England was not 'going to the dogs', but at least Hubert Podmore must have gained some satisfaction from the narrow defeat in November, 1910, of those who declared that 'public schools owe more to the playing fields than class rooms'.

In the years immediately before the First World War the public-school system was suffering from an acute crisis of confidence, a state of affairs which in part reflected broader social and political changes that were taking place in Edwardian society. The Liberal government of 1906 had embarked upon a wide-ranging series of social reforms, a development which led to the constitutional crisis of 1910–11 when Lloyd George attempted to have his 'People's Budget' accepted by the Tory-dominated House of Lords. A blow was struck against the influence and power of the Lords, as the Liberals sought to establish a new relationship between the state and the individual in the realm of social welfare. At the same time the Labour Party and trade union movement were beginning to flex their muscles and a number of militant protest groups, including the Suffragettes, were taking dramatic steps in their attempts to draw attention to their causes and establish a new political agenda. In the background loomed the threat posed by Germany, and Britain endeavoured to keep ahead of her rival in the arms race as a series of international incidents and crises pushed

Europe towards the brink of a military confrontation which would upset the balance of power and threaten the security of the British Empire. Schools could not ignore, or isolate themselves from, these developments and they were obliged to try and come to terms with a rapidly changing social and political environment.

The prevailing public-school ethos that had found expression during the late-Victorian period embraced many variants on the theme of 'muscular Christianity'. This ethos, with its emphasis on games and sermons, was dependent upon, and helped to reinforce, a broad-based imperialist ideology which was deeply rooted in the most influential sections of the political and social élite.[29] But in the wake of the Boer War débâcle, many long-standing certainties began to be eroded, and the basic principles and objectives of public-school education were called into question. The process which exposed the public schools, as well as the institutions of state, to scrutiny served to unite critics drawn from across the political and philosophical spectrum. On the one hand advocates of imperial 'efficiency' demanded that future generations of colonial administrators and senior military personnel be intelligent, enlightened individuals capable of acting on their own initiative, and writers such as Rudyard Kipling cast doubt on whether the public schools as they were then constituted could properly service the needs of the empire. At the same time, within the education establishment, liberals or progressives sought to release pupils from the rigid conformity imposed by a relentless diet of organized games and learning by rote. Standing beyond these moderate reformers were influential figures such as George Bernard Shaw and H. G. Wells who believed that the public schools were, for a variety of reasons, producing maladjusted individuals who were entirely incapable of coming to terms with the demands of the modern world. For them, tinkering with the curriculum or improving the quality of teachers would not provide the answer. Only the abolition of the system itself would remove the shadow that public schools cast across Edwardian society and, in seeking to advance their cause, Shaw and Wells launched a series of blistering attacks upon the schools and ridiculed the techniques and practices that were used to form character and educate the young. These denunciations of the system struck a chord, and Shaw and Wells attracted a large number of followers, one of whom captured the mood of the times when he wrote of public schools in the *English Review* in

1912 that 'the purpose they stand for is already obsolete; their principle is out of date.'[30] Confronted by this powerful if disparate coalition of interest groups, the public schools turned in on themselves in the years before the War and the self-confidence of the Victorian years rapidly disappeared. All schools subjected themselves to deep soul-searching as they endeavoured to adapt to a new educational and political climate in which liberals and reformers appeared to hold the upper hand.

It was in this atmosphere, a year before Louis entered the school, that Dr David began his headmastership at Rugby, and at once he embarked on a programme of reform and reorganization. Of course, many headmasters begin their tenure of office with a flurry of similar activities, all of which appear to bear the hallmarks of progress and dynamic change, but there is plenty of evidence to suggest that David had a deep philosophical commitment to the reforms he introduced. Indeed, because of the nature of these changes, one well-informed observer writing in the 1950s was of the opinion that the David era was the most interesting in Rugby's history since the time of Arnold.[31]

David was not new to Rugby in 1910: he had served there as an assistant master during the 1890s, before becoming a Fellow of Queen's College, Oxford and then headmaster of Clifton in 1904. He was well aware of the shortcomings of the school, although many others believed Rugby to be, as one observer put it, 'apparently efficient and popular, [and] devoid of any outstanding abuses',[32] and he embraced many new ideas as part of a strategy designed to breathe fresh life into what had become a rather stale and complacent institution. At this stage his ideas were not as advanced as they were later to become, but they were nevertheless radical enough to provoke significant opposition from some of his staff, a number of whom had previously been his colleagues when he had served as a competent but not outstanding junior master at the school. Moreover, he did not help his cause by criticizing existing practices, as he implied when he declared that a 'great deal of the stupidity of which masters complain is manufactured in the school itself'.[33] Such statements acted as a rallying cry for those who were frustrated by Rugby's limitations, but, as is always the case in such situations, David's methods and ideals brought him into conflict with some long-established masters who fought a determined rearguard action in defence of what they perceived as being Rugby's most cherished and valuable practices and traditions. As one insider, a newcomer to the staff, later described it, there was a 'rift in some of the old certainties, uneasiness in place of the old bland acceptance of tradition, and the gradual alignment of the staff into two groups – one conservative and rather suspicious, the other believing that it was progressive and following the lead of a reformist headmaster'.[34] This situation never developed into open hostility between the two factions, but the tensions produced by this state of affairs became the subject of a novel, *The Lanchester Tradition*, written by an influential housemaster, G.F. Bradby.[35] The novel, based upon a set of characters who were only thinly disguised, paints an intriguing and amusing sketch of life in an Edwardian Senior Common Room as a process of change begins to disrupt familiar and long-standing routines.

Whatever charges critics levelled at David, and there were many, no one could question his loyalty to Rugby or his commitment to the cause of reform. He resisted considerable pressure to move on to several prestigious posts and appointments (he later became Bishop of St Edmundsbury and Ipswich, before moving on to the Diocese of Liverpool), and he left no stone unturned in his review of all aspects of school life. Of course, his efforts were interrupted and diverted by the War, but nevertheless he did more than enough during his first four years as headmaster to leave an indelible mark on Rugby's development. One can only speculate on what he might have achieved had he been able to enjoy his tenure of office in normal peacetime conditions.

The most obvious changes made by David were those he made among his staff.[36] He was helped here by the governors' policy of purchasing boarding houses from housemasters who, in time-honoured fashion, had owned the properties they administered on the school's behalf. As a result of this, three-quarters of the houses changed hands between 1910 and 1914, and powerful and influential figures such as Robert Whitelaw, who had been a master for forty-seven years and a housemaster for thirty-seven of them, went into retirement.[37] At the same time, a cohort of young men was appointed to the staff, and they brought with them a commitment and enthusiasm which prompted one of them, who later became a headmaster, to declare that no school staff known to him had ever worked harder.[38] The administration of the school was rationalized and professionalized, the daily routine was altered, new electric bells were installed, the curriculum was updated, and as an experiment (later abandoned) attendance at Sunday Evensong was made voluntary.[39] In addition, a whole host of minor changes was introduced, many of which, like the ending of the wearing of top hats, are mentioned in Louis' letters. In the *Meteor*, the abandonment of the top hat was greeted with the remark that nothing better symbolized 'our emancipation from Toryism and of our resolution that an institution is not to be retained merely because it is an institution or because other schools retain it.'[40] Where, however, David's influence was most keenly felt by the boys was in his refusal to regard the privileges and status of prefects as sacrosanct. He made it clear to them that their positions of considerable responsibility did not place them above the law, and when senior boys overstepped the mark he did not hesitate to punish them. As Louis' letters reveal, David was determined to make all pupils accountable for their actions, and this had quite an effect on the school, none more so than when David stripped the head of school's power and privileges from him for a breach of conduct.

Above all, what marked out David from his predecessors and most contemporary headmasters was the general philosophy of education and upbringing that he attempted to apply to conditions at Rugby.[41] While organizational change was the outward manifestation of this philosophy, his whole approach to education was conditioned by the belief that schools should not be institutions based on punishment as a form of control, but that they should be places of enlightenment where personal shortcomings could be recognized, dealt with and cured on a one-to-one basis. Nothing better summed up David's general approach to his pupils than the belief expressed in print in 1932 that the 'British boy of all classes is a generous creature, open to all manner of influence that is reasonably meditated to him. Direct exhortation moves him little, denunciation less.'[42] This willingness to see good in all of his pupils stood in marked contrast to many of his colleagues, who based their house régimes on the need to organize boys for every minute of every day in order to counteract their natural inclination to seek out trouble when left unoccupied.[43]

David's ideas were advanced for his time, for he wished each of his charges, in particular the less able boys, to be allowed to develop their creative abilities to their fullest extent, and he felt

27

that this could not be achieved if their individuality was lost in the conformity and competitiveness that characterized so much of public-school life. As one member of staff put it, David seemed to offer ordinary boys a 'new deal'.[44] As an example of the headmaster's ideas being translated into action, art and craft for every boy in the middle school was introduced to the daily routine in 1914 under the title of 'manual training'. David also remained a staunch advocate of music and drama, for they also provided appropriate creative contexts in which boys could develop their individuality. Plays had been produced on a regular basis since the early nineteenth century, but David's attempts to establish a drama society were thwarted by a group of senior masters who feared the consequences of girls being invited to assist in rehearsals, and the risks associated with allowing boys to play female roles were deemed to be far too great.[45] While no one doubted the sincerity of his motives, even his friends on the staff warned him against what they regarded as a dangerous and misplaced idealism, and some of them felt that he had gone too far when he began to apply psychoanalytical theories developed by the controversial American educationalist Homer Lane to the problems of some of the adolescents under his control.[46]

David's liberal philosophy was most effectively translated into action in his genuine attempts to get to know his pupils well. This was particularly the case with those under his direct care and supervision in School House. Thus, while some meetings took the form of a formal interview and were conducted in the forbidding atmosphere of the headmaster's study overlooking the Close, many boys found their way into the Davids' home, where, for example, Mrs David held reading groups and parties on Sunday evenings. Furthermore, in keeping with a long tradition going back to the time of Arnold, domestic hospitality was offered to pupils on a regular basis and the Davids, as well as a number of masters, invited small groups of boys for breakfast and tea. In the final analysis, actions such as these might have done little to offset the generally harsh living conditions experienced by the boys, and they might not have gone down well with those who continued to preach the virtues of manliness and unsentimentality, but they helped to create a bond of respect and affection between headmaster and boys. Moreover, the new, young members of staff proved to be far more approachable than many of their predecessors, and this also played its part in transforming the relationship between masters and boys in general. Before David's arrival, staff and pupils had often viewed one another with mutual hostility and suspicion, and on the eve of the War, as Louis' letters reveal, boys still occasionally treated masters with an arrogance and contempt which reflected their mistaken belief that teachers were their social inferiors.

By 1919, however, there were clear signs that this was beginning to change, and J.H. Simpson later recalled that boys were 'beginning to talk to masters as if they were both human beings.'[47] While the trauma of the school's wartime experience played its part in breaking down these long-standing barriers, there can be little doubt that the Rugby that emerged into the post-war world was, in some important ways, cast in the mould that David had designed for it, and nowhere was this more evident than in the area of social relationships. Simpson, who endorsed and later developed many of his headmaster's methods, did not hesitate to identify this as the most significant area of change. We must be careful here because not only was Simpson a committed disciple, but he also left Rugby in 1919 before the post-war character of the school had become fully developed. Even so, he was able to argue with some conviction that 'the really important changes, more subtle and indefinable [than changes to the curriculum], all came about from the personal work of men who believed that quite ordinary boys, often not apparently doing well, had to be treated with more sympathy and personal knowledge if the best was to be made of them. We younger men felt that our headmaster cared intensely about this side of a schoolmaster's work. He was something new in our experience of public school headmasters in his capacity to make friends with quite undistinguished boys outside his own house. Not many could get to know him, but some did, and were glad that they did.'

Alongside David's progessive views, and not necessarily in conflict with them, was a continuing commitment at Rugby to a general régime based upon the principles of simplicity and hardiness. The daily routine was a demanding one, and all forms of luxury and extravagance were frowned upon by the authorities. In July, 1912, the headmaster sent a memorandum to all parents reminding them of this. He encouraged them to assist the masters in upholding and strengthening the 'traditions of simplicity and manliness upon which some of the most wholesome influences of the school depend'. Pocket money was to be restricted to a 'modest scale', and parents were asked to make life at home for the boys as simple as possible during the holidays because 'much harm is being done to health and some to character by over-indulgence in late hours, rich feeding and continual excitement, especially at Christmas time'. The school's stated aim was to train boys in the habits of 'self-reliance, and reasonable hardihood', and David stressed that he was convinced that his pupils needed 'all the protection we can give them against enervating influences of many kinds and especially those which lead to and are fostered by the expenditure of money'.[48]

The particular types of traditions invoked here by David were those which some of the more conservative members of staff believed were the very ones that were being threatened by innovation and change. For in his memorandum David was appealing to parents to help in the process of character-building, and many on the teaching staff believed that the fundamental purpose of education was to take a leading part in the development of character, not through creativity and individualism, but through the establishment of firm, well-defined behavioural guidelines that found expression in the school at large. This was the view of one of the most influential masters, G.F. Bradby, author of *The Lanchester Tradition*, who was not a conservative of the unthinking type, but rather a healthy sceptic of the type found in most common rooms. His belief, as reported by J.H. Simpson, was that 'The function of the school was to train character, and the type of character which he thought Rugby could best produce, if it remained true to its traditions, was a kind of Christian humanist of a Puritan complexion, reasonable, reticent, and a little suspicious of all enthusiasms.'[49] Bradby was aware of the dangers of attempting, as David appeared to be doing, to add new ideas to old ways, for this would inevitably dilute the basic traditions that had been in place since the time of Arnold. The result would be that Rugby would lose its distinct identity and sense of mission. Bradby stated these concerns quite emphatically when he wrote to a former colleague saying, 'I don't know whether the blend of new and old would work . . . I don't think that Rugby stands for anything in particular just now – just a hotch-potch of contradictory systems, each of which destroys what might be good in the other.'[50] Those more sympathetic to the headmaster saw things quite differently and viewed the future in much more optimistic terms, for they felt that he was retaining features of intrinsic value while reshaping the school so as to enable it to find its place in the modern world. Thus, Simpson was able to say that 'the process that I witnessed was one of humanizing and vitalizing the life of a school; of making it less rigid and formal, without necessarily making it less bracing; of increasing the dose of happiness and spontaneity, without altogether eliminating the dose of austerity'.[51] An interesting general perspective on these issues is offered in the memoirs of a boy who entered the school in 1922, the year after David was succeeded as headmaster by W.W. Vaughan. George Allen recalls that the school seemed to represent a 'blend of ancient and modern', and at the time it 'felt as though Rugby was truly in the van of progess.'[52] Whether or not they applauded the developments that took place at Rugby between 1910 and 1922, no close observers of the school could have failed to agree with the departing housemaster, Robert Whitelaw, in 1913 when he wrote, with some degree of bitterness, that the 'old order changes'.[53]

Yet for all the changes made by David in the name of progress, one has to consider the extent to which the life of any school can be shaped by the vision and actions of any one headmaster. This is particularly the case in schools like Rugby, where the institution is little more than a loose confederation of boarding houses, and where the most influential individuals in setting the standards and applying principles are the housemasters. As Simpson pointed out in his shrewd analysis of David's tenure of office, a headmaster can only show the way forward in very general terms, but for underlying changes to be made he needs the full and active support of his staff. Before David's time, headmasters of real ability and forceful personality had managed to steer a course for the school and carry the whole staff with them as they did so. While there can be little doubt that David himself was backed by many of the junior masters, it is far less certain that he gained the respect and confidence of all those who ran the houses. Life in a number of houses, one suspects, went on much as before, and if David did win a victory over the forces of conservatism then it was a very narrow victory indeed, and a price was paid in the form of concessions to tradition and the old way of doing things. Even so, if Simpson's impression can be relied upon to provide us with a reasonably fair view of what went on at Rugby during these years, then it would seem that the general tone of the school in 1919 was not only very different from that at the turn of the century, but it was also very different from that of 1913.[54] It is therefore safe to say that Louis' time at Rugby was not only a time of great change, but it covered a period when a struggle for the very soul of the school was taking place.

Lawrence Sheriff House
[Internal evidence: 29 September 1911]

Dear Dad and Mother,

I am having great fun here. There are two other chaps in my study, Bennetts and Darby.[55] This morning we were called at 7.40, and had a bath. Breakfast was at 8.15. After breakfast we had to go to chapel. The new boys had to go to the west door by 8.50. Chapel was at 9.00. There were tons of chaps. We sung the first hymn in Latin! You aren't allowed to put your hands in your pockets until you've been here one term, when you may put one in, [and] at your third term you may put both in. This is an awful bore.

After chapel all the new boys had to go to the Temple Speech Room to be tried for the choir!! My voice I am thankful to say was too deep . . .

Now goodbye,
love to all,
Your loving son Louis

Lawrence Sheriff House
[Postmarked: 2 October 1911]

Dear everyone,

I am getting on very well here. I have now begun regular work in form Lower Middle 1B. It is rather mad because I find myself just beginning to learn Greek!! whereas I first learned [it] over four years ago. The Latin, too, is very easy, and this puts me off terribly. However, I am trying to learn as much as I can though I seem to have learnt it all when I first went to St Faith's.

This morning, chapel was at 10.30. We had to wear top hats. Old Salter (the hatter) hadn't padded mine properly, so it wouldn't stick on decently. There was no sermon this morning but I expect there will be one this afternoon by the Headmaster at 4.00. Two sixth-form men read the lessons. There was a collection for the School Mission.[56] There is only a collection three times a term. The Sixth collect and the Head of the School holds the plate for the boys . . .

Mr Bullock, Mrs Bullock and Christopher (their son) have breakfast with us, the same with the addition of two little girl kids also with their governess at dinner. We (me and the five other chaps, Wright and Bennetts, in my study, and Darby, Clayton and Rosenheim)[57] have tea by ourselves. On half-hols, Tuesday, Thursday, Saturday, and every third Monday, we are allowed to make toast in our studies! Every week one of us has to cut bread at table, breakfast, dinner, and tea!!! I am the one for this week. I cut the bread quite well this morning, but you can run your finger safely along the edge of the knife. For supper we have biscuits and something which is called *cocoa*!! Over this delightful stuff we have much merriment . . .

Now goodbye,
with much love,
hoping you all flourish,
I remain,
Louis.

Lawrence Sheriff House
[Undated: early October 1911]

My dear everyone at home,

. . . Our House had to go up and see the Bidge today at 9.30. We went into his study one at a time, I 2nd . . . The Bidge asked me my name and Dad's etc; and then he asked me what I was going to be. So I said 'a missionary, I hope'. He was very bucked at this and asked me about where and when and why and how etc. He asked me if I was going up to Cambridge. I said I hoped so, and wanted to. He smiled, and said 'Or Oxford, Oxford or Cambridge? Oxford's a good place you know!' I said, 'Yes sir, my father went to Cambridge sir'. He smiled and agreed. He then asked about what House I was coming to, and said he wanted me to come to School House, and would get me in if he could. He asked me what form I was in and where; and then said he wanted me in the Sixth, and I must try to soon get there (and other rot). He is an awfully nice man [and] everyone likes him . . .

With love,
and thanking you for your letters,
Louis.

Lawrence Sheriff House
[Postmarked: 16 October 1911]

My dear everyone at home,

   . . . I have had an honour this week. Last Saturday (not yesterday) we had to write a poem on R.L. Stevenson. I enclose my effort. On Thursday when they were given back to us, Mr Mayne[58] said a lot of bosh about mine being very remarkably good, best he'd ever had, etc. etc., and then said I had to take it up to the Headmaster and perhaps he'd give me a Copy. That means that he has your name put down in an album, and if you get five Copies you get a prize. You also have CA1 (or if you have two Copies CA2 etc) put after your name in the School list. CA means classical Copies in the Headmaster's Album. Old Bullock got awfully excited about it and gave me a book of poems by Mr G.F. Bradby (a Housemaster here) called 'Reaping the Whirlwind and other poems'. This made me heartily sick as he expected me to read them. However, they are rather decent. When I went up to the Bidge (Head) he remarked that I once stayed with him, hadn't I read the thing through, and laughed when he got to the end, and said it was very nice. He asked me what of Stevenson's things I'd read, and advised me to read his letters. He then wrote A.A.D. and the date on it, as you can see for yourselves. He said he hoped he should see some more of my work.

On R. L. Stevenson

He was a friend to the poorest man
Whose heart with the wild geese goes
When they seek in the spring on their northern wing
Heedless of all but the wild things' call
The land of the northern snows.

He was a friend of the wretched soul
Near killed by an office stool,
Who longs for the light of a camp fire by night
And the eerie howl of the lone wood owl
And to learn in Nature's school.

And he had a love for the daring soul
Who would rather a burglar be
Like a cat in the dark and leave his mark
With a sporting chance when he leads them a dance
Than a whiskered grey J.P.

And he had a love for the child who sits
And digs in the sand on the beach,
Who loves so much more the wild free shore
And a pirate to be and sail on the sea
Than what in schools they teach.

. . . Old Bullock wants me to get permission to join the Natural
History Society. This includes Zoology, Astronomy, Meteorology,
Archaeology, Botany, and other 'ologies' and 'ys'. I should think it
would be quite decent. Bullock says he should like all his House to
join, even if only to back up a School institution. Will you say if I
may in your next. 3/6 damages in the bill at end of term . . .

I hope this letter is long enough.
My love to you *all*,
Goodbye,
from Louis.

Lawrence Sheriff House
[Postmarked: 23 October 1911]

My dear everyone at home,
 . . . *Of course* all the stuff I wrote was my own . . . Canon Peile
preached this afternoon. Rather a dry sermon, it was. His text was
'Whether is it easier to say thy sin be forgiven thee' etc. The point
of his somewhat lengthy sermon was that we must be good boys.
He said that as a tutor at Oxford, he had found that Rugby boys
represented the highest tone. He wasn't telling us this to flatter, it
was perhaps even to shame some of us. We, if we carried on these

good traditions, and were worthy of the School's reputation, would be true sons of it. He said he knew that it was hard to keep, at our stage, with games and things on the list, God and righteousness always with us, and to live it, but he thought a time would come when we should find it harder . . .

Now goodbye,
with love to all,
Louis.

Lawrence Sheriff House
[Postmarked: 7 November 1911]

My dear everyone at home,

   . . . On Saturday we played Cheltenham and lost. They are supposed to be the best team in England. It was quite an interesting game. We were very weak behind the scrum, although Harding at back did some very good things, and Elliott at 3/4 and Leslie at stand off half were good.[59] In the evening there was a debate against Cheltenham: 'That war is a curse to humanity'. Carried by 168–100. I voted 'Aye'. There were two Rugby and two Cheltenham speakers on each side. Elliott of Rugby was the most interesting speaker. He made us roar with his 'paradoxical aphorisms'. He spoke for the motion. Lyon[60] of Rugby who proposed was good. Elliott's idea of war [was] that 'it's only losing one's temper on a large scale'. He has a funny way of speaking, which I will show you when I come home.

I am, with much love,
Louis.

Lawrence Sheriff House
13 November 1911

My dear Mother and Dad,

   . . . Old Bullock has had lumbago for the last two or three days. This has been a great blessing as we have been able to 'play' while the 'cat' is away.

   . . . Ackroyd major,[61] Head of Dickinson's, read the first lesson in the evening yesterday. I must tell you about Ackroyd when I come home. He is, of course, a frightfully buck Head of his House, VIth, gym 20, bags, XXII cricket. Bennetts in our study, went

37

into the San. at the beginning of the term, you know, for about a week. Ackroyd was there and was most awfully decent to him, played billiards with him, and asked him to go out for walks etc, and now he always nods to him or asks him how he is when he sees him. Very decent for a sixth-form man to a new boy . . .

With love
Louis.

HALF-TERM REPORT ADVENT 1911
Headmaster: An interesting boy with some good stuff in him. He must force himself to take care about details and to do at his best level work he does not like.
Housemaster: He thinks for himself and has distinct ability in some directions. Will do better in languages shortly, I think. He seems conscientious, and *as a rule* his conduct has been very satisfactory.

Lawrence Sheriff House
[Postmarked: 18 November 1911]

My dear Dad,
 . . . It is hard sometimes to do well at work here, very hard. For you often get impots even when you know your work, as Mr Bullock himself told me yesterday, and that is very depressing to get impots.[62] And they are so dreadfully sort of after you here if you do anything wrong. But thank you very much for saying that you thought I was taking pains for it is difficult if you don't understand how hard I am trying. I do take pains very much, but as Mr Bullock says, perhaps I don't always go quite the right way to work about it.
   Well, I hope I shall see you soon now. It is Nov. 17; only 32 more days!. . .

Your loving son,
Louis.

Lawrence Sheriff House
[Postmarked: 12 December 1911]

My dear everyone,
   The Bishop [Ingham] is a very disagreeable looking, snub-nosed man, but he preached a jolly good sermon. His text was 'And he

asked what it meant and they told him "Jesus of Nazareth passeth by"'. It was chiefly a missionary sermon and rather hard to reproduce. He told us he'd lived in the African bush (he looked like it) and seen niggers take refuge under the Union Jack. He said there were such great opportunities now for missions; he said that British government in India and other places, although the natives might curse it now, would prove, though perhaps rough, a blessing, by bringing the gospel into the land. He quoted a verse of Rudyard Kipling and said 'that horrid hymn – song – of Kipling's' something about 'East of Suez, where first is same as last, where there ain't no ten commandments etc'. He said how dreadful it was that fifty-five of those who had been out as missionaries could not go back because there was not the money . . .

Goodbye; prep. stops me,
With love,
See you soon,
Louis.

Lawrence Sheriff House
[Postmarked: 19 December 1911]

My dear everyone,
    . . . Cock House match is tomorrow, which the whole lot watch. The match is the two Houses who were in the Final, against the caps and XVs in the rest of the School. Thirty a side. Lots of new caps have been made, including one for the Town!! Wonderful for the Town! Elphick[63] by name . . . By the way, Mr Bullock told me I was . . . going into the S[chool] H[ouse] next term. I am not sure whether I am pleased or displeased, as I like the House, but I think on the whole I am pleased . . .
    Hoping next time I talk to you I shall *see* you,

With love, Louis.

END-OF-TERM REPORT ADVENT 1911
Headmaster: A little sluggish, but very well disposed.
Housemaster: A satisfactory half-term in the House, and I shall be sorry to lose him. I think nervousness handicaps him in Form, as I feel he is anxious to get on.

School House
[Undated: early January 1912]

My Dear Mother and Father,

. . . I arrived at Rugby at 8.05 . . . after an amusing journey; I travelled to Bletchley in the same carriage as Spens,[64] who is one of the Sixth in SH. After that, we waited some time at Bletchley, as the train was 20 mins. late. From Bletchley to Rugby, I and the two Nuthalls travelled along in the same carriage as James, Head of Whitelaw's.[65] It was rather an unfortunate situation for the Nuthalls, as they are in Whitelaw's, but we did not see him until we had got in.

I took a cab up to SH, where sundry 'jerries' (bootboys etc.) took my bag, and I went to the matron's room, who is quite a decent lady. My box had not arrived, as I had rather feared, but I did not want it badly. I was then shown into the sick-room, where all the new boys were assembled, reading etc.: there are six others beside me. The sickroom and the library are at the disposal of the new boys until our dens are assigned to us on Saturday night. The dens, by the way, are quite the most extraordinary little rooms I have ever seen. I should think they are no longer than our dining room table is broad – simply little square holes in the wall . . .

I was next shown my dormitory, with which I am very pleased, as it is great fun, with only four of us and a Sixth man whose name is Cunningham.[66] I then had to go into the Bidge to show our health certificates, but as you told me mine was in the top of the box, which had not come, I could not show it but he did not mind. He asked me if I had been ill at all, or been to a dance with somebody who had had measles next day. I told him I hadn't been to any dances, which seemed to amuse him. After some time (at 9.25) we were all assembled in the dining hall, where the Bidge read prayers, after Clarke,[67] Head of SH, had called us over. Then we went to bed. After we had been up there some time, Cunningham came in. He did not say anything to us, but after we were all in bed, he lay on his bed and read a paper. After we had been up about half an hour or so, the lights went out, and a gentleman (butler) of the name of Busby came in and locked one of the two doors in our dorm . . .

With love to you all at home,
Louis.

40

School House
[Undated: January 1912]

My dear everyone,

. . . I don't know why Dad thinks I don't like the Bidge – I think he is an awful sportsman – easily the most decent Master here. I said I didn't like taking essays up to him. He gave me a Copy and was awfully bucked. He said it had given him a great deal of pleasure and several times remarked that it was extraordinarily good . . .

Toast fagging has started. People who have been here under six terms have to do this, but after your three terms you only have to do one piece. The process is a follows. Tea on half holiday is at 5.30. At 5.15 all toast fags rush into the kitchen (called Lep's Hole) and seize toasting forks (there are about twenty toast fags). Lots of pieces of bread have already been cut by the butler. Then you toast them before a huge fire. You bag the best part of the fire you can – the best is always 'middle-middle' i.e. the middle of the middle. If you want this you yell out 'middle-middle' or 'middle-right' or 'top-right' or 'bottom left' or 'middle-left' etc. Then when you have finished your bit you take it into Hall where you find a Sixth sitting, but you must not go along the left hand path you must go right around the table till you get to him, even if he is an inch off you when you enter the door you must go right round. Then you show him your bit of toast, turning it over so that he can see both sides. If it is black he says 'you must make another', if it is alright he says 'yes'. Then you go and put it on the table for which you are fagging. I fag for the top table. Sometimes a decent Sixth will say 'Oh you can keep that.' Yesterday Spens let me keep mine. At tea time the fun comes because the Sixth chuck the toast they don't want to our table, and it comes spinning right above your head and there is a scrum for it. I am in the best position of all for that because they always fall either on me or within my reach. I got 2½ bits yesterday. You may not scrape black off your toast, and have to make another if its too black. As a matter of fact, if you hold the toast black side down and then scrape they don't notice . . .

Now goodbye,
With love,
Louis.

41

School House
[Postmarked: 31 January 1912]

My dear everyone,
. . . Things seem to have been moving at home. What with fits, and Mr Cowen going etc. I wish I'd seen the fit, but still we had something in that way last Sunday in Chapel when a lady fainted. It was so funny. First of all a lady in the back seat right oppisite me near the little side door began to agitate – apparently the unhappy fainted lady was unconscious in her pew, and could not be moved. So suddenly, in the middle of the hymn Mr Evers (a School House Tutor)[68] simply fled across the Chapel (he sits just behind me). I've never seen anybody go so fast, walking, and [he] just helped the lady out . . .
Mr Bullock is dangerously ill. The last telegram was 'condition critical. Temperature going up'. Mrs Bullock was called to him from here. He took five hours too come round after his operation. I do hope he will be better soon, but it seems rather bad . . . On Sunday evening, several new men and last term's men went into Mrs David in the drawing room, who read to us! Doesn't it sound charming! We got no end of toffee!. . .

Now I have got to do Prep.
With love,
Louis.

School House
[Postmarked: 6 February 1912]

My dear Everyone,
. . . It is very well indeed here, but I would a deal rather be at home. Still, of course, School has its advantages.
Everyday we have CO (Call Over) three times. One at a quarter of an hour before breakfast, one at tea, and one at Dics (prayers). The Bidge reads prayers (except last night the Head man Clarke did). We have quite decent grub on the whole. My various jams come in quite useful at tea, although there is always something else besides bread and butter such as fish pudding, meat pudding; sausages there were tonight, jolly good ones . . .
Dr David had me and Selous and Lyon in to breakfast with him and Mrs [David] the other morning.[69] Selous is the son of the

hunter.[70] His father is at present in Africa, hunting. There is an excellent library here which is a very good thing. It is great fun being top of my class as I have to go on sending messages to other masters etc . . . and give out all the returned papers etc. The Sixth are a very decent set of fellows, but they are rather rotten idlers. Two of the Sixth in this House are smaller than I am, and why they should have more power than me I can't see, and nor can anyone else. There is a Sixth in every passage, and we are at the end of our passage next door to the Sixth in it, whose name is Bowyer.[71] He will be Head of the House when Clarke leaves. He is a funny man. Selous and I are continually in a roar over all the Sixth here . . . The Sixth will always do your construe for you and are very decent in that way . . . [They] can do anything they like . . .

With love to you all,
Louis Stokes.

School House
[Pencil note: 8 February 1912]

My dear everyone,

The weather here isn't, that is to say it's *piercingly* cold, the ground is about as hard as rock and it snows every now and then. There has been a good deal of skating lately, but as I have no skates and you cannot hire them, and it would not be much good if I had, and I have had several chances of playing fives, which I like extremely, I have not done any.

I have been playing fives this afternoon, it was great fun. To play fives in the afternoon you have to get the name of some Sixth man that is to say you go up to some Sixth in the Upper Bench Classical and say 'Can I have your name for a Court this afternoon, please?' Unless their name is already taken they will always give it you. You then get leave off a run and after CO you sprint across the Close to where all the Courts are. These have wire netting (very strong) in front of them. In this you stick a paper such as this 'Stokes' Court taken by himself 3–4.30, B.W. Lindsay's name'.[72] You then start playing. Now if someone else comes along who had, say, Elliott's name, who is higher up than Lindsay, he could 'dish' you, that's to say you'd have to give the Court up to him . . .

We have started fagging. I got two today – I had to take some papers to certain masters. Fagging is rather rotten on the whole.

When you hear 'Fa-a-a-a-a-g' called all the fags have to go as hard as they can to the man and the last gets it. There is an awful squash, but luckily I am a bit bigger than the majority. However, fagging does give you something sensible to do sometimes when you haven't got much to do . . .

Goodbye,
With love,
Louis.

Sanatorium
[Postmarked: 18 February 1912]

My dear Mother and Dad,

. . . I am rapidly recovering my health – so to speak, though I feel like a drunken man when I walk far. I shall probably leave tomorrow or the next day. Rev Hardwich[73] came this morning and took a short service here to about eighteen of us (there are still over sixty in the San.). This afternoon I went out for a walk with Dalton (who is coughing lowly as I write).[74]

. . . It was simply *ripping* out today. The sun was warm and everything except the hedges looked delightfully springlike. So was yesterday. There is a man in the San. who has got pneu/new/pnew/neu monia (I'm not sure about that word. I think it's the top edition – but don't quite know) he's got it rather badly I believe and has about fifty nurses. You say 'I'm glad you are being looked after properly'. You don't know Dr Simey[75] . . . It was awfully funny the first morning I stopped out. Dr Simey came into the night sickroom at S.H. and said to me, 'And what do you complain of?' I said, 'Oh – I don't know – er – sort of chill I think.' Dr S: 'I don't know what a chill is.' I thought to myself what a rotten doctor you must be then, but I actually told him the symptoms when he said, 'Ah, now I can understand.' If you could see the poor ape's face you'd understand what a baked chimpanzee he is. He was here when he was a 'boy' (lower's expression for boy) in Spiller's and was Head of the School and got his Racquet's Pair (beats everyone how he did it).

Goodbye, with love to you all,
Louis Stokes.

Sanatorium
[Note on envelope: 25 February 1912]

My dear Mother and Dad, and all the rest of you,

. . . The fellow who had _____ monia, is dead – poor chap. He died last Sunday. His name was Read – in Dickinson's House.[76] He died in here.

A man in St Hill's has caused the most tremendous excitement by running away. He is a bit off, so people think. He is McClean and lives in Glasgow.[77] He tried to go to Scotland, and was discovered on Friday, I think, in a railway carriage at Bletchley with no ticket. He has gone up to London to consult a specialist who (so the story is) has been bribed by his people to say he's mad. Should think he'd say that without any bribery . . .

Now goodbye,
With love to you all,
Louis.

School House
[Undated: mid-March 1912]

My dear everyone,

. . . I had my first experience in 'fagging out' a Sixth's den yesterday. I am fag to Bretherton[78] who is a fearful buck XV, XI, Running VIII (which he got on Saturday) though he is smaller than I am. He is a very decent man. He has a lot of beastly flowers in his den which I have to water every day, but it is not too bad, and he came in today and gave some explanatory notes as it were on them. He has two hyacinths (one double and one dark blue) and a sort of lily flower and then a lot of green weedy stuff. His den looks out on the Close . . .

With love,
Louis.

School House
[Postmarked: 24 March 1912]

My dear everyone,

. . . I went out to breakfast with Lockhart yesterday. He's a *sporty* man. We had a ripping and rather mixed dish of sausages, bacon, and eggs all in one!! He was awfully bucked to hear I came from Cambridge and lived near Fenner's . . . He said he thought Fenner's was a fine ground. He seemed to much prefer it to Lord's or the Oval.

. . . We had a good sermon today from the Bidge – on the coal strike as usual. The text was to the effect that we should 'love one another . . . to understand forgiving one another even as also Christ etc. etc.' He then showed us how we must be very careful what we say about the disputing parties especially the labourers – as they had for generations never known what it was to have the upper hand, and we cannot wonder that they may speak a little wildly, indeed it is extraordinary that there has been no violence in the last three weeks. God had not seen fit to stop the trouble yet, but he had rather belong to a country which was taught lessons in the hard school of adversity than one which had always moderate ease and success.

I hope you will hear him preach one day. He has a ripping voice – one really quite extraordinary which he raises and falls in a very good way.

. . . All fags get a cake from their fag masters next Saturday which is rather a sporting idea, at least the two fags and each sixth get a cake between them. There is going to be a collection for the poor in Rugby if the strike continues throughout this week.

I have just come back from Ma Bidge's reading, which tonight consisted of thrilling gruesome tales from Conan Doyle and Rudyard Kipling – especially suited to Sunday nights (I don't think) . . .

> Now I do not know
> of any more to say,
> so I will say
> goodbye,
> with love to you all,
> Louis.

END-OF-TERM REPORT LENT 1912
Headmaster: We shall get the best out of him soon. I am not anxious.
Tutor: Has had little chance of doing well.

School House
[Undated: early May 1912]

My dear everyone,

. . . I have got a fearfully sweaty den now . . . It is much bigger than my last one (one of whose occupants is now Clayton from Bullock's House); and there is a superior window. Altogether I am rather pleased with it. We moved in – a wildly exciting bit – last night, and it is now in fairly good order, though we still have to get one or two more things.

I am also in a new Dormitory – No 3. There are ten, counting the Sixth, in it. Selous is next bed to me. He has a den with a boy called Leonard this term.[79] But, principally, I am of course in a new form. Upper Middle Three, being its official title. Mr Hardy is my master in this form. I like him quite fairly well. I took my leave of Mr Mayne in dramatic style, dropping all the papers I had been collecting from the form and thus getting them all out of order . . .

The Bidge preached upon Health with a text about 'they say such things which go to seek a country'. His idea was that there are two ways of doing this: one in the approved explorer style, and the other by making a new country of a country. He told us how many people were dying that needn't die, daily, and it was such people as us, when we were on County Councils, Boards of Guardians, Hospital Boards, Town Councils etc. who were meant to help such (I hope I am never on one of these). Then he said how afraid he was that we should miss our opportunities etc. The sermon was mainly consisting of that sort of thing, telling us the wretched state of these unfortunate people, etc, etc . . .

> Now I have prep. to do,
> With much love and hoping you are well,
> I remain,
> Louis M. Stokes.

School House
[Postmarked: 21 May 1912]

My dear everyone,

Now really! You ought to be bucked this week. I am actually TOP of my class. Don't you call that a sweat, considering its a new class to be fourth and first in the first fortnight in twenty-three people. My report was 'very good all round'.

I have been to the bath a good deal, and my swimming is improving considerably. I played yesterday in a Young Guard game,[80] but unfortunately no one knew what anyone could do. They did not know I could bowl, so I wasn't put on. However, I actually made seven runs for the last wicket – I hit a four too! So far I have bowled in three games and taken eleven wickets . . .

With much love,
and hoping you are having a decent time.
I am
Louis M. Stokes.

HALF-TERM-REPORT TRINITY 1912

Headmaster: The tendency to neglect the dull parts of his work is serious and will spoil his chances if he is not careful.
Tutor: Has come out of his shell a little this term and is doing well.

School House
[Undated: late-June 1912]

My dear everyone,

   . . . The great thing with us has been Speech Day. I will proceed to tell you about it . . .

On Saturday we only had first lesson and then did a lovely slope for the rest. I had a Tosh[81] just before speeches which I arrived in the Speech Room for at about 11.50. Here there was a great scene. All Masters in sweaty gowns, and hats of very wild types, great fountains of blue or pink, etc. etc., while the dresses were equally vain. People kept pouring in. There was an awful squash. However at about 12.15 order was got and the Bidge rose in a gorgeous crimson and grey gown, and made a sweaty speech. He began by saying he had to review the past two years. Mentioning the list of honours gained by ORs he said one (I forget his name, an Oxford chap) had gained what perhaps was the most prized distinction of University men, namely he had been made an Honorary Fellow of his College. I suppose you see the point of my bringing this in!!!

Uncle Charlie's name figured prominently in the Coronation Honours List.[82] Then he said that many had been elected MPs – he didn't know whether at present they were to be congratulated, but at any rate the School could congratulate itself. Then he referred to Bowden Smith and Buggy Dewar who have left.[83] Then he referred to the new arrangement of work which on whole School days we have from 12.15 to 3.30 to ourselves. He finished up by saying that he was proud, and we were all proud, of Rugby, as no-one who had anything to do with it could help being. Hear! Hear! . . .

With much love to all,
Louis.

School House
[Postmarked: 17 July 1912]

My dear everyone,

. . . During this [House semi-final cricket] match [there were] rumours, which towards the end became a certainty, that the VIII had won the Ashburton. I suppose you are not familiar with the name, but it is a shield competed for at Bisley by the Public Schools, and is considered the highest shooting honour a school can get!! Of course everyone went wild with delight!! Also, we knew we should get a half! The Corps went down to meet the VIII in the evening, there [were] flags in many windows in town. Generally great excitement. At 10.05pm the Corps and VIII paraded in the Close before the rest of the School.

We were all drawn up in front of the Doctor's Wall; there were electric lights rigged up on this. After a bit the corps arrived and formed up. Then came the victorious VIII (I should mention that O.G.F.E. Breul[84] is in the VIII, he made sixty-seven out of seventy, getting the King's Cup). They stood out front shivering. Then the Corps saluted them to the playing of the Band. Then the Bidge made a funny speech. He said how awfully bucked everyone was. He had been told that he need not stay at Rugby (for he had an engagement elsewhere) as the Ashburton wasn't coming this way. But he had a [?cancellation] and was very glad to be there to congratulate them. He had seen that evening his old Corps uniform which reminded him of the days when he was as young as Mr [?] Bonboli (roars) and as innocent as Mr Podmore (bellows). 'By the way,' says he, 'before I forget I think we'll have a half tomorrow' (Loud Cheers). He then congratulated the VIII on behalf of the School. They responded by shivering, but Bonnerjee,[85] the captain, made a witty speech in which he said that when the Bidge first came with his Bride to Rugby they brought him the Ashburton as a Wedding present. This year they were performing a like benefit on Mr Hardy (cheers). They hoped, next year, they would be able to present Mr Mayne with the same present (loud laughter).

I may mention that we won it by one point . . .

Exams next week,
Love to all,
Louis.

School House
[Postmarked: 22 July 1912]

My dear everyone,

. . . Do you know I've forgotten to tell you, but we are not going to wear toppers any more after this term but are going to have special white straw hats with House colours on.

The sermon today was a fearfully tweaky one. Everyone was bucked. The preacher was an OR who had his cap when he was here. The texts were something about 'walking together in the House of the Lord as friends' . . . Then he went on to ask whether Rugby was a Christian School. 'You will pardon an Old Rugbeian asking that. I know it is a religious school, but is it a Christian school? Because however sincere our prayers are it is all to no avail if we are not learning to love all God's creatures.' He said that the spirit of unity – of love for each other was what should be aimed at. We learnt it very strongly here as each one felt he must do his best for his House and School. But were we taught to carry this into practice after we left? Most of us when we went to church never did go in the right spirit. We go to our own pew and sing our own hymns in our own way, and never look at the person in the next pew except when we brace ourselves to the supreme effort of looking round to see who's behind us and find they are singing out of tune, we never notice the rest of the people (everyone, ushers included, simply split at this but the fat little man rolled it out as if he delighted in it). It was not so, he said, here. We had the greatest opportunity of worshipping in the right spirit. We do not come to Chapel individually, we each come as part of Rugby School, and all of us worship together. The Chapel was the place to which all Old Rugbeians came to revive their memories more than the Quad or the Close. The spirit of unity was what we wanted to carry into our lives. 'And if you're not doing that; if you aren't loving God's creatures with all your heart, you might as well be playing cymbals and psalters in the orgies of Dionysius' (Audible amusement) . . .

Now I must close,
With love and much thanks to all,
from Louis.

END-OF-TERM REPORT TRINITY 1912
Headmaster: A good term. I am pleased with his development. He knows what to try for and is I believe doing his best.
Tutor: Very satisfactory. He has lost most of that peculiar reserve which made him rather unapproachable. It may have been largely due to simple shyness, and undoubtedly his ability and keenness for cricket has had much to do with its disappearance.

School House
[Undated: late-September 1912]

My dear everyone,
I arrived quite safely on Thursday night, and after a considerable period managed to get a cab with Dalton and got up here alright.

I have moved into a rotten den with Hartnoll,[86] the only advantage is the view on to the Quad. The other den overlooked the boothole.

I have moved round onto the superior side of side-tables. That is you know there are two principal tables in Hall here. One is for people 'in Hall', to which position you attain after about eight terms here. The other is for those below this position, and is called 'sidetables' [and] till you get in Hall you cannot wear double collars. Well, in sidetables, one side is very inferior and until you have attained to the far side you cannot boast to yourself of a very high position. But once you get on the other side you begin to be more important.

. . . I have got into a class which has an absolutely beastly little fellow to take it called the Rev J.M. Hardwich. He's written about a dozen books on scripture with so many notes that you hardly see the Bible-part, and he always tries to argue a thing out with you, which a master shouldn't do because he knows he can speak his mind plainly without being told to shut-up, which you can't.

This term we're going to do Physics which is Newton's fault largely. Its horrid stuff, and all about 'forces'.

I can't see the good of lessons at all. Who cares a half-penny what Caesar did in Gaul? I think lessons are very dull things when you've got an usher like Mr Hardwich. However, luckily it is great fun in the House . . .

Goodbye,
Very much love to all,
Louis.

School House
[Postmarked: 6 October 1912]

My dear everyone,

. . . I am getting on rippingly here. I am very glad in most ways that I came to Rugby, and now I'm here I know that School House can't be beaten – it's ripping. I have no end of fun, and if it were not for the fact that I like a more what do you call it kind of existence, but still it is grand here.

. . . Have just come back from a Lockhart stodge with Selous and Lyon. He is a *topping* man. He knows such a deal and is awfully decent. Though he is very keen on games he says that if now he were to start his 'varsity career again and had to choose whether he would play games or devote the time to learning music, he would learn music, and you know he is a double Blue. We ragged him about this, but he was firm that music is a joy to you long after football and cricket days are past. We had a long discussion on this point . . . He is very down on the state of our football here: he says there's not a man in the School that's got any idea how to play!! We had great fun . . .

Excuse awful writing,
It is a pain to write with such a pen.
Great haste,
Love to all,
Louis.

My dear Dad (and others),

. . . You may remember that there is an absolutely new football scheme on now, which is causing considerable excitement. It's meant to revive the ancient glory of rugger here; for, according to Lockhart 'there's not a man in the School who has any idea how to play Rugger.'!! The scheme is this: that twice out of three 'halfs' in a week special games shall be played, not by Houses but by size and merit, so that you get a game which is much better, for everyone is more equal, and of the same size. Also there are referees to each game. There are eight school games, ranging from game one the highest. I played in game four today . . .

Much love to all of you,
Goodbye,
Louis.

School House
[Postmarked: 24 October 1912]

Dear everyone,

. . . Today we had our first House match, and when you consider what it means to have the School XV Captain on your side, you will see how simply *rotten* for us it was to lose him, especially as he is awfully good. Of course as the accident happened on Tuesday his thumb wasn't well enough for today, and so we had to turn out without him (I wasn't playing. You see I play wing 3/4 and as both wing 3/4s are School Distinctions – well – you can hardly expect me to – but I hope I'll play for the 2nd XV). Then, if you please, in the first two mins one of our best 3/4s broke a tendon in his ankle, and has to go off the field! Groans! Moans! Oh! We fought hard and grimly, but they got over (this is an expression for scored) twice, then we got over once. At half time we were 8–3 against us. Hoyle (the injured 3/4)[87] came on again, but almost immediately went off. After this, though we fought hard every inch of the way, they got over several times and half way through the second half we saw that we were beaten, but we still played well. It was dreadfully hard luck. We can safely say if Leslie and Hoyle had been playing we should have won, almost comfortably. Of course we're terribly down, but its worst of all for Leslie.

As for the explanation of all these accidents, it merely is that you can't play Rugger without them, [and] if you saw a good game you'd understand. For instance Leslie's thumb – he was just kicking the ball up and one of the other side not unnaturally tried to prevent him, but I think even then he might have done something less ferocious than kicking hard at his hand! The wonder is that there aren't more. For instance, one frequent cause is this: when a pack of eight heavy forwards are rushing the ball with their feet down the field, the only way to stop them is to fall on the ball. In doing this you will see that accidents are unavoidable. You may be kicked in the eye, nose, mouth, ear, stomach, kidneys, ankle, anywhere, and the whole eight forwards may all fall on your arm and break it. You see you must keep the ball, it's the only way. But all this is by-the-way, part of the game.

> With love,
> Goodbye,
> from Louis.

HALF-TERM REPORT ADVENT 1912
Headmaster: We expect much of him and he must look after himself accordingly.
Tutor: Has plenty of originality and spirit, and should do well. But he ought to have the sense to work without pressure.

> School House
> [Postmarked: 24 November 1912]

My dear everyone,
. . . We watched the Uppingham match. This is one of the three matches which the whole school watches: i. The O.R. match. ii. the match v Cheltenham or Uppingham (one year we play them on their own ground and the next year on ours) and iii. the match against the Town.

I am sorry to say Uppingham won 11–3pts. which was really rather a good performance for us considering two of our best men were not playing owing to injuries. It was a good match to watch. The difference between their men and ours was considerable. They're all a bit loud, don't you know. They wear bright things

1. + 2. Two early photographs
of Louis Stokes with his father, the
Rev. Henry Stokes.

3. Louis while a pupil at St Faith's Preparatory School, Cambridge.

4. The family in 1913.

5. Louis (seated right) in his first year at Rugby. His Housemaster, the Rev. Llewellyn Bullock, and Mrs Bullock are standing at the rear.

6. Rugby School Second XV, 1915. Louis is standing second from right. The insignia on the jerseys indicate the boys' boarding houses.

etc. There was some absolutely splendid tackling by our fullback, de Selincourt.[88] He brought his man down most beautifully. Tomorrow, winter hours start, i.e. we get up about $\frac{1}{2}$ an hour later in the mornings . . .

END-OF-TERM REPORT ADVENT 1912
Headmaster: I don't mind high spirits, but he is much too good a boy to let them get the upper hand at the wrong times. I don't like the record of those two weeks.
Tutor: He is very different from what he used to be, and is frankly high spirited. I do not think he is really lacking in energy, but has a cheerful way of at times doing as little as he is allowed to.

School House
[Postmarked: 26 January 1913]

My dear Dad and Mother,
   . . . I wonder how many people get prepared for confirmation by a Rugger International in the same year as he plays? J.H. Bruce Lockhart is playing stand-off half for Scotland against Ireland on Feb. 1st.[89]
   Our new form master Mr A.P. Cox[90] is a very foolish young man. I do not approve of him at all.
   . . . It is unfortunate that Mrs Vinter should have selected Stallard's [for her son], for really, of the Houses proper (that is not counting the Town House) it is quite honestly the worst. It really is a shocking house – a set of hooligans in it for the most sort, though one or two are nice chaps. Low in games, untidy looking, and the food!! Words simply fail. However as I suppose you will have to answer Mrs Vinter you can say food – wholesome and simple; Life – very easy; nice companions etc . . .[91]

I remain,
Your very loving son,
Louis M. Stokes.

School House
[Postmarked: February 1913]

Dear Mother and Dad,
   . . . I went out to tea on Monday with a weird master called Mr

J. Farrell.[92] The J stands for Jerome . . . He is very interesting to talk to, he is a strange young man, he has people round to his rooms to say their work when they have done it badly and gives them sticks of chocolate. He gave another boy 2/6 to buy a cone with – telling him to keep the change – the boy bought a cone for 1d.! He talked to me for a long time, he wanted to know what I would like to do instead of Latin and Greek, so I said I should like to do gardening or something like that. He was very serious about it . . .

Goodbye with love,
Louis.

[Included with this letter is the following typed note sent to the Revd Stokes by R.S. Goodchild, the Assistant Secretary of Cambridge University Appointments Board on 7 February. This note was part of a letter that had been sent to Goodchild by Farrell.]

3 Bilton Road,
Rugby,
6 February 1913,

As to a private matter, I have just made the acquaintance of your friend Stokes in Upper Middle 1 which I take for Greek. It is a subject against which he has a grievance as being inferior to gardening, but he is a bit of a poet and an intelligent talker. His scowling smile is very quaint. At one time I thought he might be inclined to play upon his supposed stupidity and act the buffoon for the benefit of his young companions, but we have made friends over a cup of tea and he is not now inclined to pose as the misunderstood victim of our obsolete educational system – at least not with me. He wrote some really good verses about P.L.S. [sic] about four years ago but is ashamed of them now because some of the masters rotted him about them – a perfectly unnecessary precaution because the boy is not conceited.

Believe me,
Yrs sincerely,
Jerome Farrell.

HALF-TERM REPORT LENT 1913
Headmaster: Thoughtful and honest. Very good progress.
Tutor: Excellent in every way, except that perhaps it still requires a little persuasion to make him really work. He is so capable of thinking for himself however that he ought to grow out of that.

School House
[Internal evidence: 2 March 1913]

My dear Mother, Dad, etc., etc.,
    . . . We had the most fatuous sermon I've ever heard this afternoon from Spitter's brother.[93] It mainly consisted of a very vivid description of the last lap in a race, and various hints on how to run in general based on St Paul's remarks about keeping your body in temperateness in his Epistle to somebody. Everybody in Chapel roared the whole time. We do get some awful specimens here. They have, many of them, yet to learn that we know a good deal more about it than they do . . .

Goodbye,
Shall see you soon, what ho!
Love from Louis.

School House
[Undated: March 1913]

My dear Mother and Dad and others,
    . . . I had a talk with Dr David the other night about confirmation. He sent for me, and asked me various questions, one of which was what I said in my prayers. However, I was prepared for this so I wasn't quite knocked out.
    He told me that when one asked one's sins to be forgiven it was better to go over them each separately. He said, 'And remember, Stokes, it's always a continual warfare – good against evil not good people against bad people mind you – but good forces against bad forces – always a warfare', and he seems to rather impress that on us in the talks in Chapel – that it's a warfare.
    Don't you think it somehow makes it rather bitter – and not truly happy – if you are feeling 'I am fighting' and not 'I am loving' or 'trying' or something else? I can't quite reconcile myself

to the idea of fighting – it doesn't seem to be what is meant in Christianity . . . Oh! dear this ecclesiastical news – it is dreadful having to relate everything. . .

With love to you all,
I remain,
Louis M. Stokes.

School House
[Postmarked: 24 March 1913]

My dear everyone,
    . . . The Confirmation service was, as you say, very impressive indeed – very, but I must say that it seemed – at least I didn't much like the Bishop. P'raps it was because I sat right under his nose. It's hard on these occasions to feel properly about things – still he gave a very good address.

He said that as he had a bad cold and was in danger of losing his voice before the end, he would give all his address beforehand – instead of in two parts. The best things he said were that we weren't going to say 'I think' or 'I feel' or 'I want' or anything like that – we were going to say 'I do' and that must be the keynote of our religion – a religion which does something for us and others.

Then he said that a motto which all through life we might take and write it down in our prayer books and look back to it in after years – when things went against us – was 'Faith and courage'. Faith to simply believe in Christ. Courage to help us to follow him truly, and then we were confirmed.

Afterwards I felt a somewhat depressing reaction – but in the evening I had a tremendous fight in our House Boxing Competition against a man nearly two years older – a ripping fight it was – simply topping – and though he beat me on points the Gym instructor said I wasn't to be expected to win as he was about a stone heavier and a good deal taller.

This fight made a great difference – it seems funny that it should have done – anyway I felt much more real after it. Borrow, you know, says in Lavengro in his famous 'Life is sweet, brother' passage 'Come and put on the gloves with me brother – and I will try and show you what a thing it is to be alive.'
    . . . Thank you for the book – which is nice and the tract which is nice too, but I'm afraid I don't much appreciate that kind of

58

poem which it is based upon, because here at Rugby you aren't sentimental, no one tackles better than Rugby men, no one anywhere plays a better game – cricket or footer – but you don't say anything. Still, some people like that kind of poem . . .

Goodbye with love,
from Louis.

END-OF-TERM REPORT LENT 1913

Headmaster: I am sorry to read this report. I had a much higher opinion of him. I can only hope that next term he will change his attitude. This is quite unworthy of him.

Tutor: Rather unsatisfactory. If, as seems certain, such good work is only inspired by fear of punishment, it shows great want of pride and self respect. He has been stupid to tell himself that it is useless to work at anything which does not seem likely to be of distinct service to him; and though not by nature a slacker he has little interest in most of his work.

School House
[Undated: May 1913]

My dear Mother and Dad etc. etc.

. . . I went to Holy Communion this morning before breakfast – it was a nice service, and afterwards to a Lockhart stodge which was frightfully dull. Lockhart never knows what to talk about, and there are long and dreadful silences. He's an awful little man in that way. However I expect he is in a ghastly funk as he is shortly to be married and is planning out a great honeymoon, and the builders who are building the house he and his wife are going to live in have gone on strike, so he's having a most unhappy time of it . . .

Goodbye with love,
from Louis.

HALF-TERM REPORT TRINITY 1913

Headmaster: I have respect for many of his qualities, and I believe he understands what is needed – a firmer hold for himself and his thoughts.

Tutor: Though very satisfactory in some ways, he is getting to an age where common sense and self respect might with advantage play a bigger part. Pressure is still needed for good work.

School House
[Internal evidence: 18 May 1913]

My dear everyone

. . . Yesterday was rather amusing. Crowds of men and boys from the Rugby Mission Clubs in Birmingham and Notting Hill came down at about 11 o'clock. They had dinner in the various houses. Then an eleven of theirs played an eleven of ours and all sorts of rags happened. After tea they played a football soccer match against us, [the] score was 1–1. I don't know who won the cricket. I know they were jolly good. They also gave exhibitions of sword play etc. in the Gym. At 7.45 there was the annual meeting in the Temple Speech Room. The Bidge made a characteristic speech, and introduced a chap called the Rev Sheppard. He has worked for the Club a good deal and gave us a most amusing speech. He was rather funny looking – a round face with a broad grin and black short hair. He told us several amusing stories. Once he was preaching on New Year's Eve in East London and the church was crowded with all kinds, people who had just come out of pubs. One man came in and yelled 'Good evening guv'nor' to him, so he said good evening and asked him to sit down. So he did and kept quiet till the end of the sermon when he suddenly jumped up and said 'What I say is – Vote for Tariff Reform' (it happened to be election time).

Another tale was that a lady wanted to help the poor a bit. So she went visiting in her carriage in East London. She called on Mr Jones and said 'Oh I'm sorry I haven't been able to come before, you know my daughter has just come out and I've been so busy bustling round after the dresses and things.' So Mr Jones said, 'Well now, that's a funny thing – my son's just come out. How long did your daughter get?' . . .

With love to you all,
Louis.

School House
[Internal evidence: 25 May 1913]

My dear Mother, Dad, and others,
   . . . Today is about 300 degrees in the shade. I have left off my waistcoat and am still melting.
   Mr Paine is more hopeless than ever.[94] He knows no Latin whatsoever and never gives papers on our work, always just a few viva voce questions. It is a toss up whether one is high or low for the week with him . . .
   This afternoon we had a sermon from Rev H.H. Symonds, a Master here (an OR), a shocking sermon it was.[95] 'I will not fear what man can do unto me for the Lord is on my side.' In talking about public schools he said that the strength of the School lay in whether it cared more for industry than cricket. Games, he said, were necessary and good and healthy, but had no moral value at all. More battles were lost than won on the playing fields of Eton.
   There's fine sentiments for a Master of Rugby School! I wonder how far, if at all, you agree with him. Everybody said afterwards what a rotten sermon.

With love to you all
Louis M. Stokes.

END-OF-TERM REPORT TRINITY 1913
Headmaster: He has certainly a considerable gift of composition. I want him to be ashamed of doing badly – he can do so well.
Tutor: He is doing quite well in work which is most unsatisfactory and shows complete absence of self respect. He should be ashamed to leap up in form as he has done at any threat of punishment only to sink again. But he has shown what he can do and he must hold to it next term.

School House
[Postmarked: 28 September 1913]

Dear leader [sic],
   . . . I am in the lower VIth. My form master is the Revd J.M. Hardwich . . . It is much nicer in the Upper School – as I am now because (i) we don't have weekly marks (ii) you don't have to fag (iii) you can make toast for yourself.

However, one has to do what are called 'copies', that is twice a week certain work out of school has to be done – a Latin prose and verse. Still it might be interesting. There are lots of new Masters – most of them awfully stupid looking. There have been several airships down near here but I could not sweat to go and see them as they were a mile or two away and it has been very hot . . .

Love to all,
from Louis.

School House
[Postmarked: 26 October 1913]

My dear everyone,
    . . . I have had a bad week with J.M. Hardwich – he is in many ways an extraordinarily objectionable gentleman. I should almost be inclined to think that he had quite forgotten that he was a boy himself. He looks at everything from his own learned and dreadfully scholarly point of view and *never* by any chance *attempts* to help anybody with their work – oh! that's not his mission he thinks, his particular line is to shout himself purple in the face over the least mistake anyone makes – he would be really disappointed if we weren't so bad as he makes us out to be. Its a real joy for him to nag away at people.
    Now Mr Raven and Mr Hardy and Mr Lowe (at St Faith's) taught you decently – they try to make you learn something – they don't want to make any error in translation a butt for their wit – they assist – and educate not shout and bore as Mr Hardwich does . . .

Yours with love,
Louis.

HALF-TERM REPORT ADVENT 1913
Headmaster: It is bad for him to be continually doing less than his best. He must wake up.
Tutor: There was never any reason why he should not become a person of some culture, but he must pull himself together very sharply as his present course seems likely to lead in the direction of somewhat childish 'uncivilization'.

School House
[Postmarked: 3 November 1913]

My dear everyone,

. . . Yesterday the School team played a very hot team of ORs including R. W. Poulton (SH OR) Captain of England XV for 1913 (who said Rugby doesn't produce good players?) Kenneth Powell (the hurdler) who plays for the Harlequins, R. Cunningham who plays with Poulton for Liverpool, F. C. Bourne who boxed for Oxford etc.[96] The School were ahead 21–14 at half-time, but the age of the ORs told in the second half and the final score was about 39–26 against us. Poulton scored a wonderful try from his own 25 . . .

Yours,
L. M. Stokes.

END-OF-TERM REPORT ADVENT 1913
Headmaster: I am delighted with this immense step forward. Now his many good qualities will have free play and development.
Tutor: His half term report seems to have had the effect of bringing him into line again from every point of view. I hope his success will have given him a new inspiration for work. That is what he needs.

School House
[Postmarked: 25 January 1914]

My dear everyone,

. . . I have at last settled down into barmaids [sic], a den to myself, and a new dormitory; and am very well pleased with all my surroundings etc. and shall hope to put in a good term's work. I should here say that I am in a different class; I got my remove after all; I may as well remark while I am about it that this class is called the middle Vth, but you need not try to remember this as I can quite easily tell you again some time next holiday.

My present Form Master is Mr St Hill.[97] Goodbye – forever I trust – to the Rev Manisty Hardwich. Dr David preached his usual poor sermon today; and we all sang the usual 'Lord behold

63

us with thy blessing, once again assembled here' and as usual looked forward to the day when we shall sing 'Lord dismiss us with, etc'.

My den looks very nice; but after all your trouble I have decided not to have any pictures up as I think it looks nice without; besides which I am of the opinion that pictures are not conducive to hygiene in that they collect microbes, nor to work in that they distract the mind.

I should like here to thank all those who contributed to my provisions; for which I am very thankful – and pleased with them . . .

I remain,
Yours very truly with love,
Louis M. Stokes.

School House
[Pencil note on letter: 6 February 1914]

My dear everyone,

I am very sorry that my letter is so abnormally late. I should explain that the higher you get here in work the more there is to do, so much so that I have no time except on Saturdays and Sundays and sometimes Fridays to write; there is a lot of work which is to be done out of school hours, so that as I did not write on Sunday this is the first real chance I have had. I have now fallen into the old régime; up you get at 6.30, down into Chapel across into School, do Thucydides as in a dream, back to breakfast. After breakfast one begins to awaken.

However, my Form Master this term is quite excellent. While he sees that the work is done, he never nags at you as Mr Hardwich did, and it is done the more readily therefore.

I have been getting on quite nicely. I am in Mr Lockhart's German set and he is one of the stupidest men to learn anything from I ever struck; not a single person in the set knows more than 5 words of German and Lockhart rattles out great questions in German, and flies into disgraceful fits of temper if you ask what he said. However German is only twice a week.

. . . You will be pleased to know that Mr Raven's reading society has broken up owing to lack of support; personally I am not sorry

– as I always went more because I couldn't exactly say no than because I liked it.

I hope Dr David will be in good form; anyway I think you'll like the look of him; he's a very good man indeed, but you will probably find him terribly vague; he tries to say such very hard things – I think too hard for the majority of people here to understand. Certainly so in my case . . .

Wishing you all love (whatever that means)
from Louis.

School House
[Postmarked: 8 February 1914]

My dear everyone,

 . . . I go for 'Bigside' runs now. Perhaps you don't know what these are. Well, there is a Running Cup which is annually in the Spring Term competed for by the House. Every Tuesday there is a Bigside Run of 6–8½ miles. Every person who comes in *within ten minutes* of the first man home counts 10 points for his house. The House which gets the most points wins the cup for that year. We got it back last year, but I could not run as I wasn't sixteen (you are not allowed to run unless you are sixteen). There is tremendous keenness about it. There have been two runs so far, on both of which I came in all right – well within time with about three minutes to spare.

Now I must say
Goodbye with love to all,
Louis.

School House
[Postmarked: 17 February 1914]

My dear everyone,
 . . . Time is slipping away. It is Half Term come next Saturday.

I am very pleased with myself this week because I came in twenty-fifth in the last Bigside Run which doesn't sound very high at first sight but when you remember what a lot of people there are it is quite high. On Tuesday I hope I shall be higher still . . .

I went out to breakfast this morning with Lyon to the master who teaches me French, Mr Whitworth,[98] who was at Cambridge and knew Mr Goodchild – and whose brother was once Lyon's private tutor. He's a very nice chap indeed – very simple and doesn't know a word of French – so we get on well.

I am making very distinct progress in German – with the help of (and in spite of) Mr Lockhart . . .

Yours with love,
Louis.

School House
[Postmarked: 22 February 1914]

My dear everyone,

. . . We had a most hopeless sermon this afternoon by the Principal of St Edmund's Hall (wherever that is). He made such a noise that nobody could get to sleep either, except a certain Mr Donkin[99] who is a master here – sitting just near me – who managed it beautifully. (Do you remember by the way the Donkin who coxed the Oxford boat for four years about two years ago? It was his son I believe, and he always tries to bring this son up if you enter conversation with him; he is dragged up regularly.)

A frightfully funny incident has happened this week; at least funny for all except the victims. The Head boy of the School (who manages all the School accounts with the groundsman and the School farm – and is Editor of the School mag. and generally runs everything) has, with various other of the Sixth in his House, got into a frightful row; apparently they climbed through a trap door in a bathroom with squirts, and, making their way along the roof, descended by another trap door into another dormitory and squirted all the delighted youths. Then very suddenly the matron appeared, found the whole dorm swimming in water, went and fetched the Housemaster (Mr Steel)[100] who of course was simply white with rage; next day they were sent up to Dr David who has taken all their Sixth power away for the rest of their time here; which means that they are just become like ordinary boys again with no privileges, and subject to the rule of the other Sixth. It caused great excitement here; as although other Sixth have had their power taken away before now (two in SH last term) yet never has the Head of a House, much less the Head of the School, suffered such an indignity; not the least funny part of the whole thing is that the person who is second in the School – and now of course becomes Head – has himself had his Sixth power taken away from him for climbing in at a window after lock up. Indeed he only got it back last term . . .

Hoping you will all keep as I am,
With love from Louis.

HALF-TERM REPORT LENT 1914
Headmaster: A good place. I want him to be very ambitious.
Tutor: Good. He is doing better everywhere and giving more satisfaction to everyone.

School House
[Postmarked: 1 March 1914]

My dear everyone,
    . . . I must tell you that we had Commander Evans last Tuesday.[101] I have very seldom heard anything that was so interesting; I thought he spoke commendably simply; when there was a picture of a Siberian pony and a man in its stable thrown on the screen he just said, 'The man on the right is an Eton boy – Captain Oates'. Captain Oates looked like a tramp. The lecture really was wonderful; while the pictures were just as good; everybody was awfully bucked. It was funny I thought that Commander Evans was the last man to shake hands with Capt Scott, and here he was at Rugby safe and sound. But he had an exciting time. One of the most interesting things was the way they talked of nothing but food after a bit on their journeys; and planned out great feasts when they got back to civilization. I can imagine it very vividly . . .

Goodbye with love to all,
Louis.

School House
[Postmarked: 8 March 1914]

My dear everyone,
    . . . I have told you I believe that we were having Board of Trade Inspectors down last week; they have gone now. It was rather interesting; scarcely a lesson went by but in popped an Inspector. 'Oh! May I listen for a minute or two?' 'Oh! do – we're

just having an English lesson – the boys prepared it last night, and they're being asked questions now . . . yes Milton – *Paradise Lost* – certainly' etc. etc. The Inspectors I may say always came and sat by me because on the other side of me there was an empty seat, so I used to move up (every time it used to be: the master: 'Now you move along Stokes'. The Inspector: 'Oh! don't pray move for me'). I always used to hide my notebook when I heard the knock on the door, so they didn't get the chance to inspect my work. Mr G.F. Bradby, by the way, got rather jolted by one. He explained to the Inspector that he had dictated some notes to his class on some scripture. A little bit later the Inspector said, 'May I see these notes?' 'Oh', says Mr Bradby, 'I haven't exactly given them them yet, but I'm intending to'. . .

Love to all,
Louis.

END-OF-TERM REPORT LENT 1914

Headmaster: He still needs too much watching and stirring, and the Scripture result is disappointing.

Tutor: Though otherwise satisfactory, he has failed to keep up his improvement in work. His readiness with excuses and to blame anything or anyone but himself inevitably convinces one that his heart is not yet in his work. In the few hours where I take him I have had one or two glaring instances of failure to apply his brains to his method of tackling his work.

School House
[Postmarked: 10 May 1914]

My dear all,

. . . There is nothing except work doing here, and that I do not make a report of. Cricket of course is going along as usual, but though I am still playing I am not taking it seriously in any sense this year, as I'm spending all the evening buried in my books in quite a scholarly style. I quite laugh to see myself sometimes, but I get through a good deal in the end. Incidentally, I have been doing rather well in what cricket I have played with 25 not out and five or six wickets, and I played for the 1st House XI, all through the pouring rain too on Thursday afternoon when it poured for an hour and, under some extraordinary new rule that seems to have been made, we had to go on playing, in one thin shirt which could not be changed, to 5.45. – it was very wet and cold fielding from 2.30–4 and then sitting watching other people bat from 4–5.15 . . . However [it was] quite as interesting as some other things – and yesterday it really was quite amusing – so cold that we played in overcoats!!

Love to all, Louis.

School House
[Postmarked: 14 June 1913]

My dear Mother and Dad,

. . . There is some excitement here over mumps which has broken out to the extent that Speech Day has been cancelled for good, and they expect a lot of cases – about 200 between next Saturday and the 25th, at least that will be the first batch probably; then there may be another lot about a fortnight later and so on.

There was a masters' meeting to decide whether we should be sent home or not; the motion seems to have been lost. Anyway, I don't intend getting mumps; those who will get it will be the ones who aren't in training: I am and I shan't get it.

. . . I saw my report. Lockhart was very nice about it. He said it was a pity that the old tale about not taking pains at uninteresting things was dragged in, but he thought that this time there was something to be said on my side. He said several times, 'Yes, I think it is very creditable.' He finally said 'and I'm glad you've got into the House side' . . .

Love,
Louis.

HALF-TERM REPORT TRINITY 1914

Headmaster: Good. His high spirits just enough restrained are a delight. He is working very well, but I want to see some more English pieces.

Tutor: In one case at any rate (German) he has taken pains with what did not interest him, with the result that he not only has done well but also found a liking for his subject. He is in the highest of spirits, not too high, I am glad to see, for work.

School House
[Postmarked: 29 June 1914]

My dear *all*,

. . . Well, on Wednesday I was frightfully bucked because I have been put on XXII ends; this is Greek to you. Let me explain. XI is the first cricket distinction here; then the XXII which means that you are among the best XXII people in the School. The XI and the XXII have of course special 'ends' (the Rugby term for nets) to practise at. Well a few people (only three others besides me) who have not got their XXIIs are allowed to bowl on these ends whenever they like. This is called being 'on' XXII ends; meaning that although you haven't got your XXII you are sort of a candidate as you may say in that direction. I am as you may imagine wildly bucked; I can go and bowl there whenever I like to the School XI or anybody (pom pom hurrah!). I am afraid there won't be much work done by Stokes on Wednesday afternoons; however, believe me I am trying desperately hard to stretch to the standard of the 1st half at work . . .

Love to all,
Louis.

School House
[Undated: July 1914]

Dear All,

. . . I shall never forget the shriek that went up all round the ground as the last bails went clicking off [in the Cock House match against Hawkesworth's] and we'd won by 40 runs, and as we walked in all School House on either side of the pav. cheered and cheered and cheered and cheered. Then when we came into tea in the evening (the House XI when they are Cock House have to walk in late) the whole House cheers and thumps and shriek and break plates and spoons and knives as the House XI, feeling very pleased but extremely foolish, walk in to their places.

Again, in the evening, after prayers, the whole House files into the Quad for 'Quad chairing' in which the House XI one by one are carried on shoulders around the Quad while everyone cheers. This is a very painful proceeding and those who are wise use even their fists to escape the triumphal ride as you are dropped hard onto the paving at the end of it. I was wise.

After this you go into Hall, and a panel in the wall is taken out and from the wall [is taken] a little tin box inside which are written on little lists the names of those who have played in Cock House XVs and XIs since about 1870, all the great names such as Yardley, Bradby, Cave, and Clayton etc. etc. Our names are duly written out and interred among the great. Pom! Pom! . . .

Love to all,
Louis.

END-OF-TERM REPORT TRINITY 1914
Headmaster: Very good. He has been doing first rate work again.
Tutor: A most excellent term, full of bodily and mental activity. He has brought much enthusiasm into everything he has done.

NOTES TO PART ONE

1   H.H. Hardy, *Public School Life. Rugby* (1911), pp.19,23. This
    book appeared as part of a series on the public schools. It is a non-
    critical work, somewhat akin to an official extended prospectus, but
    it contains much of interest on the minutiae of Rugby life. Henry
    Harrison Hardy was an assistant master between 1905 and 1919
    before becoming headmaster of Cheltenham College. He served in
    the Rifle Brigade and General Staff CSO3 during the war. He was
    awarded the MBE and was twice mentioned in despatches.
2   J.H. Simpson, *Schoolmaster's Harvest. Some Findings of Fifty Years,
    1898–1944* (1954), p.72. J.H. Simpson was a pupil at the school
    between 1897 and 1902. He returned as an assistant master in 1913
    before leaving to become headmaster of Rendcomb College. During
    the war he served in the Grenadier Guards. His memoirs provide a
    valuable insight into the school from the point of view of both pupil
    and master.
3   Ibid.
4   Ibid.
5   Evidence from the 1880s suggests that most boys leaving Rugby
    went into careers in law or business. Comparatively few went into
    the armed forces, overseas service, politics, or administration (Bam-
    ford, *Rise of the Public Schools*, p.210), but this might simply be a
    reflection of family origins and backgrounds rather than a reflection
    of any dominant ethos within the school.
6   Simpson, *Schoolmaster's Harvest*,p.69
7   A.J. Meadows and W.H. Brock, 'Topics Fit for Gentlemen: The
    Problem of Science in the Public School Curriculum' in B. Simon
    and I. Bradley (eds.) *The Victorian Public School: Studies in the
    Development of an Educational Institution* (1975), pp.103–4.
8   Simpson, *Schoolmaster's Harvest*, p.69.
9   This description of the organization and content of the curriculum
    is based upon the pamphlet produced by the school for parents,
    Educational Course (1911), and Hardy, *Public School Life, passim.*

10 It has been calculated that in 1906 the modern side and the army class combined accounted for about 40 per cent of the boys in the school (J.R. de S. Honey, *Tom Brown's Universe: The Development of the Victorian Public School* (1977), p.138).

11 Simpson, *Schoolmaster's Harvest*, p.59.

12 David, *Life and the Public Schools*, pp.17–19, 24–8.

13 Roger Abbot Raven was appointed as an assistant master in 1910. He left Rugby in 1927 to become a lecturer in Education at King's College, London.

14 Simpson, *Schoolmaster's Harvest*, pp.120–1.

15 The memoirs of Robert Collis confirm that a great deal of time in class was spent learning facts and being tested (Collis, *Silver Fleece*, pp.51–2).

16 Ibid., p.135.

17 Ibid., p.65.

18 Simpson, *Schoolmaster's Harvest*, pp.65–6.

19 Hardy, *Public School Life*, p.76. The details of games organization used in this paragraph have been gathered from this source. For a sketch of a low-standard house match of 1914 involving four Tibetans representing Town House see Collis, *Silver Fleece*, p.25.

20 Simpson, *Schoolmaster's Harvest*, p.61.

21 Hardy, *Public School Life*, pp.71, 79. For a contemporary description of just how important house matches were to boys at this time see Collis, *Silver Fleece*, pp.57–9.

22 Throughout 1912 the school magazine, the *Meteor*, commented on the low standard of football over the previous fifteen years, and various reforms and ideas were discussed. The Old Rugbeian England international, Ronald Poulton, wrote a letter to the *Meteor* in June 1912 pointing out that other schools produced players of a much higher quality. He suggested that the abolition of house matches might be necessary before the overall standard of play in the school could improve. Poulton (SH 1903–8), later Poulton-Palmer, won 17 caps for England between 1909 and 1914. He was killed at Ploegsteert Wood in May 1915 while serving with 4th Bn, Royal Berkshire Regt.

23 Simpson, *Schoolmaster's Harvest*, p.61.

24 Ibid., p.71.

25 Ibid., p.51. For a discussion of militarism and military training at public schools see P. Parker, *The Old Lie: The Great War and the Public School Ethos* (1987), pp.34–5, 55–6, 61–2.

26 See Louis' letter of 7 November, 1912. This debate was held after the school's football match against Cheltenham. Speakers representing both schools spoke for and against the motion. Unusually, this particular debate was not reported in the *Meteor*.

27 Hubert Podmore who was at the school as a boy between 1901 and 1906 joined the staff as an assistant master in 1910.

28 Simpson, *Schoolmaster's Harvest*, p.125.

29 Much of the rest of this paragraph is based on E.C. Mack, *Public Schools and British Opinion Since 1869. The Relationship Between Contemporary Ideas and the Evolution of an English Institution* (New York, 1941, reprinted 1971), pp.177–302.

30 Quoted in ibid., p.277, n.30.

31 Simpson, *Schoolmaster's Harvest*, p.130.

32 Ibid., p.117.

33 Ibid., p.121.

34 Ibid., p.116.

35 George Fox Bradby (OR) was appointed an assistant master in 1888. The author of many books and poems, he was a housemaster between 1908 and 1920. His brother, Henry Christopher, was appointed an assistant master in 1892 and was a housemaster between 1910 and 1925.

36 The reforms mentioned in this paragraph are described in more detail in J. B. Hope Simpson, *Rugby Since Arnold* (1967), pp.158–64.

37 The rather acrimonious circumstances surrounding Whitelaw's retirement are detailed in ibid., pp.161, 164–6.

38 Simpson, *Schoolmaster's Harvest*, p.111. Fourteen new masters were appointed between 1910 and 1913.

39 For David's account of the Evensong experiment, the reasons behind it, and its eventual abandonment see *Life and the Public Schools*, pp.202–7.

40 The *Meteor*, 30 July 1912.

41 David's ideas were very much an exception to the general rule among leading headmasters at the time. See Mack, *Public Schools and British Opinion*, pp.426 n. and 435 n.

42 David, *Life and the Public Schools*, p.110.

43 For a good example of this type of organization in the previous decade see Simpson, *Schoolmaster's Harvest*, pp.57–8.

44 Ibid., p.122.

45 Ibid., p.64.

46 This episode is examined in Hope Simpson, *Rugby Since Arnold*, pp.183–5.

47 This paragraph is based upon, and the quotations are taken from, Simpson, *Schoolmaster's Harvest*, pp.126–7.

48 David's memorandum of July 1912.

49 Simpson, *Schoolmaster's Harvest*, p.117.

50 Ibid., p.119.

51 Ibid., pp.126–7.

52 George Allen, 'Rugby in the Twenties: the School and Cotton House, 1922–7' (typescript, 1993). George Allen's memoirs contain many interesting insights into the life of the school as it recovered from the experience of the war years.

53 This sentiment was expressed in a printed letter Whitelaw sent to all his friends when he retired in 1913. This version is to be found in the copy of Hardy's *Public School Life* held in the Temple Reading Room at Rugby School.

54 Ibid., pp.127, 132.

55 Maurice Bennetts (SH 1911–15): served with 3rd Bn Welsh Regt; awarded MC. Cyril George Darby (G.F. Bradby's 1911–15): served with U Battery, RHA, 4th Cavalry Division; awarded MC; wounded.

56 The school had two mission clubs, one in Birmingham, the other in Notting Hill. The club in Notting Hill still survives.

57 Roger Benjamin Bickley Wright (Stallard's 1911–14): served in the Grenadier Guards; wounded. Wilfred Henry Clayton (SH 1911–15): served in the Royal Navy. Trevor Felix David Rosenheim (H.C. Bradby's 1911–15): changed name to Rose in 1914; served in the RHA; wounded.

58 Cyril Mayne taught at the School between 1907 and 1912 before going into the Church.

59 Leslie O'Brien Harding (Whitelaw's 1907–12): served in the Rangoon Mounted Rifles. Ian Frederick Lettsom Elliot (St Hill's 1907–12): served with 4th Btn Suffolk Regt, Machine Gun Corps; wounded. Oswald Edward Henry Leslie (SH 1908–12): served with 234th Siege Battery, RGA; awarded MC; wounded.

60 Percy Hugh Beverley Lyon (Steel's 1907–12): served with 6th Bn. Durham Light Infantry; awarded MC; wounded and taken prisoner in 1918; later headmaster of Rugby (1931–48).

61 Thomas Noel Ackroyd (Dickinson's 1907–12): served with 1st Bn Bedfordshire Regt, having previously been invalided out of the Sherwood Foresters; killed at La Coulette on 23 April, 1917.

62 Impots.= imposition, extra work.

63 William Roy Elphick (Town 1908–12): served in 108th Infantry, Indian Army; died of cholera at Bombay on 7 June, 1916.

64 Thomas Patrick Spens (SH 1908–13): served with the 5th Bn Cameronians; awarded MC; wounded.

65 George Robert Falkiner Hans Nuthall (Whitelaw's 1911–14): served in the RGA. Winfred Lawrence Falkiner Nuthall (Whitelaw's 1911–15): served in the RFC; awarded DFC. Bernard Ashworth James (Whitelaw's 1907–13): served with 13th Bn Middlesex Regt.; killed at Delville Wood on 18 August, 1916.

66 Rupert Vincent Cunningham (SH 1908–11): served with 25th Bn Liverpool Regt.

67 William Hamilton Clarke (SH 1906–12): served with 3rd Bn Worcestershire Regt; killed at Spanbroek Mollen, Flanders on 12 March, 1915.

68 Claude Pilkington Evers (OR): appointed assistant master in 1902; housemaster 1919–1935.

69 Frederick Hatherley Bruce Selous (SH 1912–15): served in the RFC; awarded MC; killed over the German lines on 4 January, 1918. Malcolm Douglas Lyon (SH 1911–16): served in 37th Brigade RFA; wounded.

70 See below, pp.182–3.

71 John William Bowyer (SH 1909–13): served with 13th Bn Rifle Brigade; killed near Arras on 10 April, 1917.

72 Bernard Wilfrid Lindsay (SH 1908–13): served with 2nd Home Counties Brigade RFA; died on 22 November, 1918, of wounds received near Kerkhove.

73 Reverend John Manisty Hardwich: appointed assistant master in 1899; housemaster 1913–1929.

74 Charles Henry Chesshyre Dalton (SH 1910–14): served with 5th Bn Northamptonshire Regt and 20th Btn Lancashire Regt.

75 Athelestane Iliff Simey (OR): School Medical Officer 1908–30; served in RAMC.

76 Brian Henderson Read (Dickinson's 1909–12): died in School on 18 February, 1912.

77 Walter Alexander MacLean (St Hill's 1910–12): served with 1st Bn Black Watch; mentioned in despatches; wounded and taken prisoner in 1915.

78 John Talbot Bretherton (SH 1908–12): served in several regiments; mentioned in despatches; awarded MC; wounded three times.

79 Gordon Hare Leonard (SH 1912–14): served in RNAS and RAF.

80 Young Guard=Junior team. The Old Guard were, and still are, teams made up from members of staff.

81 A tosh=a swim or bath. The Tosh was the swimming pool.

82 Charles Tertius Mander was created a Baronet in the Honours List of 1911.

83 Philip Ernest Bowden-Smith (Steel's 1905–9): served with the 19th Hussars; wounded. Ian Dalrymple Dewar (SH 1907–11): served with the 5th Bn Cameron Highlanders; wounded twice; killed in France on 16 March, 1918.

84 Oswald George Frank Eustace Breul (H.C. Bradby's 1910–13): served as a motor cycle despatch rider in the Royal Signals; awarded MC; died from illness at St Omer on 16 October, 1917.

85 Krishna Kumar Edwin Bonnerjee (Whitelaw's 1908–13): served in 6th Bn Royal Sussex Regt and RFC.

86 Amyas Victor Hartnoll (SH 1911–14): served with 98th Brigade RFA; awarded MC; wounded.

87 Humphrey King Hoyle (SH 1908–13): served with 5th Bn Royal Lancashire Fusiliers; killed at Gallipoli on 7 May, 1915.

88 Aubrey de Selincourt (St Hill's 1908–13): served in the RFC; taken prisoner in 1917.

89 Lockhart, who played club rugby for London Scottish, did not in fact play against Ireland. He did, however, play against Wales in 1913 and he won a second cap against England in 1920.

90 The name of A.P. Cox does not appear in the School Register which suggests that he had been appointed on a temporary basis.

91 Geoffrey Odell Vinter entered Stallard's, by then run by Charles Hawkesworth, in 1915. He left after only two terms to go to Clifton, a move which suggests that Louis' assessment of the house was a fairly accurate one.

92 Like A.P. Cox, Jerome Farrell appears to have been appointed on a temporary basis.

93 This would appear to be a reference to the sermon preached on 2 March by the Reverend D.E. Shorto. Shorto had been on the staff since 1898.

94 Paine appears to have been appointed on a temporary basis.

95 Henry Herbert Symonds preached his sermon on 25 May. Symonds was an assistant master at Rugby between 1912 and 1922. He then went on to become headmaster of King's School, Chester, and Liverpool Institute School.

96 Kenneth Powell (Michell's 1899–1904): represented Britain in the Hurdles at the Olympic Games of 1908 and 1912; served as a Private with 1st Bn HAC; died on 18 February, 1915, of wounds received near Ypres. Robert Cunningham (SH 1903–8): served with 10th Bn Liverpool Regt; awarded MC and mentioned in despatches; wounded three times. Frederick Chalmers Bourne (Collins's 1905–10): served with 4th Bn Royal West Kent Regt.

97 Edward Ashton St Hill: appointed assistant master in 1895; housemaster 1910–20; left Rugby in 1927.

98 Eric Edward Allen Whitworth: appointed assistant master in 1913; housemaster 1924–8; then headmaster of Bradfield College; served with 2nd Bn South Wales Borderers; awarded the MC and Croix de Guerre; twice mentioned in despatches; wounded.

99 Arthur Edward Donkin: appointed as an assistant master in 1875; housemaster 1884–1910; retired in 1920.

100 Charles Godfroy Steel: appointed assistant master in 1878;

housemaster 1891–1914; died in 1921 while still teaching in the school.

101 A detailed report of Commander Evans' lecture on Scott's polar expedition is to be found in the *Meteor*, 20 March, 1914, pp.16–18.

PART TWO

RUGBY SCHOOL AT WAR

August 1914–December 1915

At the end of the Summer Term, on 28 July, 1914, the Rugby School Officers' Training Corps had departed for their annual Summer Camp at Cannock Chase, Staffordshire. An outbreak of mumps had reduced the attendance from an expected two hundred to only sixty-six, and, despite the glorious weather, 'there was a tense feeling in the air the whole time'.[1] The international situation had been steadily deteriorating since the contingent had arrived at Camp. Austria had declared war on Serbia, and Germany had declared war first on Russia and then France. In time-honoured tradition, the Regular Army had decided that it would soon need to march on its stomach, and recalled all the cooks from the Camp on 3 August, followed immediately by all other regular troops. On 4 August half the tents and half the blankets were similarly required by His Majesty's Troops, and 'it became evident it must be war'.[2] The Camp broke up two days early, the pupils returning home on trains crowded with soldiers who had been mobilized and were rushing to rejoin their units. War had been declared at midnight on 4 August, 1914.

When the Advent Term began on 24 September, 1914, one pupil described returning to a 'very altered school';[3] many of the older boys and some of the younger masters had left Rugby. Robert Collis thought there was 'a new air about the place', and that the school 'passed through a unique period during the next four years'.[4] There were thirty fewer boys in the school in September, 1914, than there had been in the previous July, and by October seventy-two Rugbeians who had left between January and July, 1914, had joined up.[5]

Rugby was, of course, not alone in providing large numbers of old boys for the war effort; every public school in the land could point with pride to vast numbers of volunteers, and later casualties.

Those who had been educated in 'a gentlemanly tradition of loyalty, honour, chivalry, Christianity, patriotism, sportsmanship and leadership'[6] were ideal officer material, especially to lead a vast new volunteer army with only a minimum of training. Such codes of behaviour, emphasized first by Thomas Arnold at Rugby and later disseminated throughout the public-school system by former pupils and colleagues, were an ideal preparation for war. The tragedy was that they had not been prepared for the particular war being waged in 1914 which 'brutally exposed the inadequacy both of an out-moded set of ideals and an archaic and optimistic concept of warfare'.[7]

However, to the pupils of 1914 the principal concern was that the prediction of many politicians and soldiers would be proved correct and that the war would indeed be over by Christmas. Ernest Raymond's often quoted lines in *Tell England* summed up the mood:

> Eighteen, by Jove! You've timed your lives wonderfully, my boys. To be eighteen in 1914 is to be the best thing in England . . . Eighteen years ago you were born for this day. Through the last eighteen years you've been educated for it.[8]

Rupert Brooke[9], Old Rugbeian, had written in 1914:

> Now God be thanked Who has matched us with His hour,
> And caught our youth, and wakened us from sleeping.[10]

By the end of 1914 it was calculated that 1,650 Rugbeians were serving in the armed forces, which was seventy per cent of those eligible to do so.[11] They had not been denied their opportunity to get in on the show.

Whatever the hopes of his pacifist father, when Louis returned to Rugby in September, 1914, he was to be continually reminded of the War, and subjected to subtle military-patriotic pressures and influences, which were later to lead him to enlist. Rugby was far from being an overtly militaristic school before the War, but there were still links with the armed forces which could not be ignored. At the end of the summer term in 1914, for example, four pupils passed into Woolwich and five into Sandhurst; there was an army class in the school, spread across four year-groups, numbering forty-seven pupils; there was a voluntary Officers' Training Corps with approximately two-thirds of the school enrolled. In 1906 compulsory drill and shooting for the whole school was introduced, which even for non-members of the Corps was one hour's drill per week and a termly shooting test. Inevitably, once war was declared, the atmosphere changed markedly. The editorial of the first school magazine of the Advent Term 1914 boldly declared: 'Rugby is well and nobly represented in the armies of the Empire; and it lies within us to find new Rugbeians to replace the fallen. Many of us here now will take their places in one or two terms' time; nor so long as men are needed will Rugby fail to send her sons'.[12]

Prior to 1914 the OTC had been for most boys an opportunity for open-air activity rather than serious military training. The OTC had succeeded the Rifle Volunteer Brigade in 1908 as part of Lord Haldane's plans to establish a Territorial Reserve Force; the War Office financed the OTC and laid down regulations for its training. There were weekly parades, compulsory field days, NCOs' classes, and also classes for those wishing to take Certificate A, an examination of proficiency introduced by the War Office. This involved a practical test in drill and commanding a squad, and also a written examination. During the War Certificate A was 'a passport opening all doors to a Commission.'[13] The OTC was organized on House lines, and consequently competitions in drill and tactics were keenly contested. Shooting was a very important part of the OTC and the Rugby VIII had been highly successful in winning the premier public-school trophy, the Ashburton Shield, in 1907, 1909 and 1912. When the triumphant Rugby VIII returned in 1912 the entire Corps was on the station to meet the team. A representative of the Town Council went to meet them and gave a speech; the Corps Band, the Church Lads' Brigade and the Bugle Band then escorted them to the Close, where the local territorial unit and hundreds of spectators were waiting. Speeches were given, the school and national anthems were sung.[14]

Annual inspections, introduced after 1908, were a consequence of War Office funding. In 1910 the contingent was described as being 'in a very efficient state'; in 1911 as 'a thorough and workmanlike body'; and in 1913 as being in a most efficient condition, and 'a great credit to the Officers' Training Corps'.[15] Annual camps had become increasingly popular in the early years of the twentieth century, with 170 Rugbeians attending Summer

Camp on Salisbury Plain in 1911, 194 at Bordon in 1912, and 163 again on Salisbury Plain in 1913. David's predecessor as headmaster, Dr H. A. James, had evidently seen the virtues of Camp and had joined with the headmasters of Eton, Harrow and Winchester to send a circular letter to all parents in 1909. It requested parents 'to make such arrangements as you can that the boys may feel their attendance at the Camp is a real engagement demanded of them, not a mere school matter, but as a duty to their country'.[16] The OTC saw it in a different light from the headmasters, being a case of 'willing sons, unwilling parents; keenness enough and to spare'.[17]

However the War Office and the Commanding Officers saw the OTC, for the vast majority of pupils it was nothing more than an enjoyable break from the treadmill of the school timetable. Field days were described as 'agreeable picnics, memorable just because they were breaks in the normal routine, and took us right away from school'.[18] Gervas Huxley, a pupil at Rugby from 1908 to 1912, found field days 'enjoyable occasions', which were made the more so by the discovery of, 'the devastating shrapnel effect of firing a round of blank ammunition into a large cow-pat'.[19] Robert Collis thought 'no English O.T.C. ever made anybody militaristic or taught him anything about modern war.' He concluded, 'the whole business . . . is merely so much waste of time.'[20]

With the advent of war, however, the OTC took on a new importance in school life, and this is fully shown by Louis' desperation to join. There were two full parades a week and many hours given over to drill, route marches, scouting, musketry, trench warfare and any kind of physical activity which would train for endurance.[21] The extra time needed for these activities, calculated at fifteen hours a week by Collis, was taken from games. As hundreds of Rugbeians began to join the War, the OTC felt able confidently to justify its position: 'There have been those who derided the O.T.C. as playing at soldiers; but their derision is strangely silent now.'[22] Within the first fifteen months of the War, twenty-thousand young men with OTC experience had been granted Commissions, enough to officer over five hundred and seventy battalions.[23]

Gervas Huxley recalls a major scandal while he was at Rugby. It concerned the behaviour of two senior boys who reacted against what they considered the excessive zeal of the Commanding Officer of the OTC in ordering some extra parades. They removed the buttons from their uniforms, and gave the lack of these essentials as their excuse for not turning out on parade. When it was discovered that the loss had been self-inflicted, the whole Corps was paraded and in a 'scene reminiscent of Dreyfus's epaulettes of rank being publicly removed', the culprits were made to stand forward and were commanded to leave the Corps which they had disgraced.[24] Such seriousness, though not reflected by the majority of Rugbeians, would undoubtedly have accorded with the intentions of the War Office in setting up the OTC. It is a measure of how important the OTC was in providing officers, that the Commanding Officer, C. P. Evers, was Mentioned in Despatches in March, 1918, although he had never left Rugby. William Blunden suggested that the OTC was 'an influence directing the world in its limited way, out of the paths of peace'.[25] William Plomer, the poet and novelist, a pupil at Rugby in 1917–18, enjoyed the experiences of the OTC. His biographer, however, maintained that the OTC was a 'direct preparation for death in the trenches'.[26]

Perhaps the type of officer who was thought to be produced by the Rugby School OTC can be gauged from the writings of Donald Hankey[27], Old Rugbeian, who wrote under the pseudonym of 'A Student in Arms', in *The Spectator* in 1915-16. Hankey had enlisted as a Private, and in an essay entitled 'The Beloved Captain', described such an officer as:

> Tall, erect, smiling . . . at the start he knew as little of soldiering as we did . . . he was learning his job, and from the first saw that his job was more than to give the correct orders. His job was to lead us . . . he watched every one of us for our individual characteristics. We were his men . . . and he was our leader . . . He had a kind of innate nobility which marked him out as above us.[28]

Inevitably the war also took its toll on the teaching staff. In July, 1914, there were thirty-six full-time members of staff and 555 pupils.[29] By December, 1914, five members had joined up and, to a pupil of the time, this gave the impression that 'most of the younger masters had left'.[30] In total nine masters joined up before the end of the War, and three were to lose their lives.[31] The young, energetic and fit were replaced by a variety of part-time and temporary teachers, which led many pupils (including Louis) to complain about deteriorating standards of teaching. In 1917 Rugby temporarily employed two female teachers for the first time, which clearly shows just how severe was the shortage. Other gaps in the teaching staff were filled by those previously retired, such as the Reverend William Payne-Smith, who had been a housemaster from 1895 to 1902. Rugby School, like many other employers, guaranteed the employment and seniority of those who left for the war. A list of masters, published each term, was ordered strictly on length of service in the school. The then financially lucrative posts of housemaster only went to those at the top end of the list, and so it would have been an important factor that masters maintained their seniority, despite being away at the War.

The temporary staff were pejoratively known as 'war-substitutes' and the pupils 'waged an incessant war'[32] with them. Collis describes one altercation with a temporary master, which led to the whole form being set ten thousand lines. He led a delegation to the headmaster, who sided with the pupils, saying, 'the master in question was leaving at the end of term'.[33] Alec Waugh, a pupil at Sherborne, published a fictional memoir of his schooldays. He wrote, 'all the young masters have gone, we are left with these fossils fretting because they are too old to fight, and making our lives unbearable because we are too young.'[34]

Louis would also have been confronted by the War in numerous other ways whilst at Rugby. For example, there were frequent lectures on military topics, which, although voluntary, were attended by a large proportion of the school. In October and November, 1914, Hilaire Belloc lectured twice on 'The Strategy of the War'; in January, 1915, H. Gregorius Brown lectured on 'Austria, Hungary and the War'; in July, 1915, A. H. Pollen lectured on 'The British Navy at War'; and in October, 1915, Dr V. Cornish lectured on 'The Strategic Geography of the War'. Even the Natural History Society was affected by the need for a military sounding title, with a lecture billed as 'Weather Records in Peace and War', given by R. Lempfert.

The School Debating Society, which Louis regularly attended, similarly concentrated on military topics. In November, 1914, the motion was 'That arbitration is not necessarily preferable to war as a method of settling international difficulties' (For 37, Against

7. Louis Stokes in the uniform of the Royal Marines Light Infantry.

8. Royal Marines Light Infantry, Gosport, February, 1916. Louis is bottom right.

9. Louis' grave in Mailly Wood Cemetery.

10. The Royal Naval Division Memorial at Beaucourt.

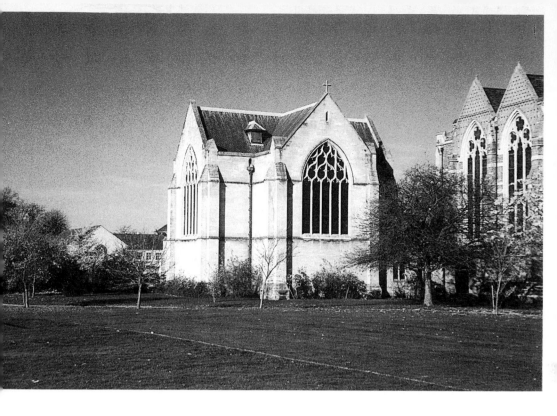

11. The Memorial Chapel, Rugby School.

12. Part of School House, Rugby.

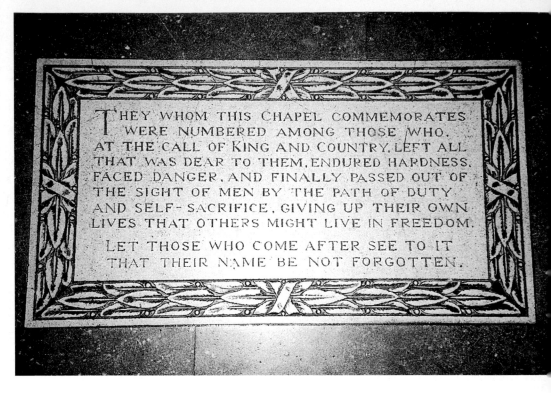

13. Floor tablet in the Memorial Chapel, Rugby School.

14. Wall tablet in the Memorial Chapel, showing the names of some of those killed in the Great War, including that of Louis Stokes.

56); in February, 1915, the motion was 'This house censors the Government for its censorship of the Press, its failure to introduce conscription, and its treatment of recruits and soldiers' dependants' (For 4, Against 69); and in November, 1916, the motion was 'That the conscientious objector has been very unfairly treated' (For 19, Against 54).

Regular memorial services were held in the school, beginning in November, 1914, to commemorate the Old Rugbeians who had died in the War. The *Meteor* became increasingly a publication devoted to lists of those serving in the War, and details of those who had been killed, wounded and decorated. At noon every day the Chapel bell was rung and all classes were halted for a time of quiet prayer for those at the War. Many sports fixtures were played against the local billeted troops and there were Belgian refugees in the town. All this kept the War at the forefront of Louis' mind.

Another aspect of school life which changed, undoubtedly for the worse, was the food. No public school was noted for its cuisine, yet as the German U-boat campaign began to take effect the standard of food deteriorated even further. In 1917 William Plomer remembered, 'little slices of chilled meat, a small quantity of doubtful bread, and a few spoonfuls of sugar'.[35] After a full morning's work on a winter's day, lunch consisted of 'a little slop of bony, oiled fish and a dab of watery custard'[36], followed by a long run in the afternoon, and work again at night, with perhaps only two slices of bread to keep one going. Plomer blamed the 'semi-starvation' at Rugby for his ruined eyesight which forced him to leave the school after only one year.

The food shortages became so acute in 1918 that the townspeople of Rugby were starting to get aggravated at having to share their limited food with an influx of hungry boys. As a consequence, the Levée passed a rule that no food was to be bought in the town by the boys of the school.[37] As compensation for the shortage of food, the whole school was allowed an extra half-hour in bed in the mornings.

The War lurked around every corner for Louis' generation of public schoolboys. It was not just the constant reminders as friends, team-mates or even fag masters, perhaps only a few months senior, were killed, maimed and wounded at the front. It was also the realization that there could be no gradual attainment of manhood; the complete responsibility of adulthood was thrust upon them in the form of an army uniform as soon as they left school. Louis, like thousands of other public schoolboys, responded to the patriotic call to do his duty. The traditional emphasis of the public schools on fair play, self-sacrifice, strong leadership and bravery were seen to be the ideal preparation for officers leading the new volunteer army. The Army was much like public school[38] so it was no surprise that many attacks on enemy lines were led by an officer kicking a football into no-man's-land. They were playing on the muddiest games pitch in history in the 'Greatest Game of All'.

School House
[Postmarked: 25 September 1914]

Dear Dad,

Here I am back in school and having great fun.

I *must* join the O.T.C. Corps only I must have your signed permission. I enclose the necessary.

Pray don't deny this as absolutely everybody without exception is flocking to join, and I do want to and David seemed awfully pleased at my doing so, and at others. . . .

Now goodbye
love to all,
Louis.

School House
[Postmarked: 28 September 1914]

Dear all,

. . . Dad's picture will go up when I find a piece of string for it. Otherwise I don't know that I intend adorning my den in any other way unless I buy a picture of Admiral Jellicoe or somebody and stick it up, which perhaps I shall (opposite Napoleon) . . .

I am in Mr Jack Collins'[39] form, who is a desperately funny man, and makes the most extraordinary personal remarks, of which I will give you samples at a later date . . .

I saw a paper today (given me by a master) in which E. F. Boyd[40] and A. O. Boyd[41] (both O.R.s) are respectively killed and wounded. It seems to be a terrible struggle on the Aisne. A boy here (Porchester[42]) whose uncle has come back (wounded at Le Cateau) says his uncle said that he with 2,000 others were captured by the Germans, mostly wounded. The doctors were very good to them (German doctors, of course), and shared their food with them, and finally when the Germans began to retreat and they had to leave them, they put up a notice to the British Commander: 'Here are 2,000 of your wounded. We have done all we can for them, and hope you will do the same by our men in a similar position.' Signed, Royal German Medical.

This is the kind of thing that does *not* receive a headline, or even a paragraph in the left-hand bottom corner of the back page in the papers.

Mother made no mention of the O.T.C. I asked about. I suppose the letter came all right. I hope it is receiving due attention . . . I must rush and read Samuel 1–7 chapters, for Divinity tomorrow.

Love to all,
Louis.

School House
[Postmarked: 4 October 1914]

Dear all,

. . . A Belgian refugee turned up here the other night and wanted to know how to reach the monastery there is here. So Dr David called Porchester . . . and asked him, as being the only person at School House Rugby who can speak French at all fluently (he speaks pretty well), to interpret to this good gent and take him to the monastery.

So Porchester took him along. On the way the poor man told him how he had been one of the chief engineers at Louvain, and had of course fled with the rest. 'Ah my poor sons, where are they?' he said (in French of course). He said that the Belgians were very frightened of the German heavy artillery, especially as the guns in all the forts in Belgium are of an antiquated style . . . and were not much use.

Suddenly, he put down his bag, leant up against the wall of the street and began to cry, 'Ah my poor country! Ah my beautiful town! My poor sons, where are they?'

This went on for some time. The wretched Porchester of course didn't know what to do; he tried to comfort him by saying, 'I'm dreadully sorry for my poor sir; *we all have these terrible hardships*,' which last seems to me an extraordinary form of consolation to offer. However, we'll hope he did not notice it. Suddenly Dr David came along on his bike, riding to the monastery. So he gets off and came up, and Porchester explained what was happening. They let the poor man cry on and Dr David told Porchester that the man had brought a picture . . . of his six sons, and drawn his fingernail across the neck of one to imitate that he had been killed.

Eventually the gent cheered up a bit, and they went on. He said he thought Porchester was a French Master, but Dr David eagerly assured him (in broken English) that he was a pupil. So he asked if Porchester learnt his French at Rugby, of coure Dr D[avid] would have liked to have said he had, but Porchester gets it from his mother who is half French . . .

However, he was very pleased with Porchester on the whole, and said it was wonderful how well he talked and he didn't wonder the man took him for a Master etc, etc.

Today the Belgian came to dinner with David. Porchester was invited. Dr David knows practically no French; however, he thought he'd have a try. So beginning to carve the mutton he says to the Belgian, 'Voulez vous de mouton?' The wretched Beigian didn't know what to say. He spluttered and hummed and said it was very kind of Dr David but he hadn't any where to keep sheep. At this, Mr Raven (one of the S.H. tutors) who was present, and talks French fairly well, began to roar with laughter and explained to Dr David that he had asked the Belgian if he would like to keep sheep.

Dr David said, 'Ah yes! Yes! First effort, first effort,' and being told by Mr Raven what to say, said it. . . .

The Chapel bell tolls like ours at twelve everyday; it tolled yesterday just as I was being asked a question I didn't know. By the time the prayer interval was over, I had had time to find out, so I was saved. 'It's an ill wind . . .'

Goodbye. Love to all,
Louis.

School House
[Undated: early October 1914]

My dear Dad,

Thank you very much for not standing in the way of my joining the Corps. Dr David told me what you said about it, and I see exactly what you mean; I don't think I am likely to become infused with the spirit of militarism.

Dr David said you seemed to think that I ought to have showed him your letter to me; he asked me to clear up any impression you might have that I withheld the letter wilfully when it would have been better to show it him.

In your letter to me you said that if Dr David or anyone said anything, I could show them that letter.

Just above that you said, 'you must say that, while your father holds that the present opposition to German militarism is right, he looks forward to a different condition of affairs, and that he is President of the Cambridge Arbitration Association which anticipates better things'. It seemed to me a poor objection to my joining the Corps, for I suppose most people 'look forward to a different condition of affairs'.

You gave no reason that I could understand why I might not join; you went so far as to cast aspersions on me by saying, 'I hoped that you would have been brave and refused it on your own initiative'. When I say that it was on my own initiative that I applied to join, any idea of 'braveness' seems rather out of the question.

Further, as at the end of the letter you admit that you have had to write it in a great hurry, I could not believe that the letter would be the best explanation that I could give to Dr David. So I said to Dr David that you did not want me to join as you 'were for peace' . . . although you agreed with the motives inducing us to enter this war; further, that you were afraid that the Corps was 'military'. He said, 'Yes, I expect that's what a great many of them are afraid of; that's the difficulty.' I added that I thought you possibly did not quite understand about the Corps. He then offered to write to you about it, for which I thanked him and left it at that.

From this you will be able to judge whether or not I put the case fairly. If you think I did not, I am sorry. When Dr David

92

mentioned later that you thought I ought to have showed him the letter, I offered to.

Apart from this point, which I have only dwelt on because Dr David asked me to, I do believe that it is a very good thing to be in the Corps. The influence you can have on the others is very much helped when you join in everything.

So again thank you very much, more especially as perhaps you would rather I was not in the Corps. I hope it will benefit me in many ways, and harm me in none.

With love,
Louis.

School House
[Postmarked: 11 October 1914]

Dear Dad,

I have thought over my letter and your comments on it, and I am bound to say that I agree with you that it was a bad letter and, as such, I am sorry I wrote it . . . But there is one point, the most vital, which I should like to clear up. Namely with respect to the following passage in your letter of last week, 'it is of great regret to me that you do not agree with your father.'

It would naturally be a regret to you if I were not to agree with you that war is wicked; but I do agree most thoroughly with you on that score.

But what I do think is that war, simply as war, is only the outcome of wrong things in people. And I think that those wrong things find issue in so many other ways besides war that it is misleading to place war apart from other wrong things, and magnify the importance of 'the wickedness of war'. If you like to call it the 'wickedness of selfishness', that is alright. Because war, that makes people die and makes people homeless and sad, seems to me no worse than peace which allows many people to die, from want of money to cure them (when that money is spent by those who have plenty of it, on racehorses for instance) and which allows people, in thousands, to wander homeless, and others to have homes that *we* should not like to live in. It is obvious that you know more about these last things (London slums etc) than I do. Then I think that it is a pity that more prominence is not given *not*

93

to the wickedness of those who want war, but to the wickedness of *all* those who don't want 'thy kingdom come'.

Isn't it largely because war appeals to the feelings so much more than other forms of wickedness that it is held up as so bad. (And it is bad). You say, 'look at the money spent on Dreadnoughts – wasted'. But look at the money spent on racing, theatres, etc, – wasted. 'Look at the lives wasted in war,' people say. Look at the lives wasted every day in peace. Of course I know you know all this; and I'm not setting up to teach my grandmother to suck eggs or anything. I'm only stating (rather badly) why I think that war is treated rather sentimentally and out of proportion. Probably I have put down what I mean very badly; I think I have. But what I mean is right, I am sure.

I take it that you are afraid that I might develop into 'an unsettled young man', and that is why you did not want me to join the Corps. I hope I shall do no such thing. Why I wanted to be in the Corps (and I am glad I am in it, and again thank you for allowing it) is because any influence (to use a horrid word, but one which you will understand what I mean by it) one can have here is greatly helped if you are in the Corps. Because here there's no militarism in people's ideas attached to the Corps. It is looked upon as the one and only bit of 'manual labour' or 'active service' you get here, and as such – I mean as something you can *do* – I think it is good. I don't agree any more than you do with great armaments, but I do think at this time it is a good thing to show actively, that any strength you have you will give to fight rotten ideas like the Germans have.

Hoping you will endeavour to see the spirit more than the letter of this letter.

I remain, with love
Louis.

School House
[Postmarked: 18 October 1914]

My dear all,
I fear those who hoped the war 'might be over by Christmas' will be disappointed. It looks as if Lord Kitchener, with his 'in the

94

event of the war lasting for more than three years,' is nearer the mark . . .

Porchester went up to London yesterday about his teeth, and there he met an uncle of his who was wounded at the Marne I think. They told him that in the Connaught Rangers eighteen out of twenty-two officers have been killed, while the K[ing's] O[wn] Scottish Borderers (Amos' Regiment) is practically non-existent; the same with the Munster Fusiliers. He says they say the trouble about these Belgian refugees is that a lot of them are German spies.

The sailors are said to be getting very jumpy. They don't like waiting by Heligoland etc., with nothing happening. A fellow called Clayton (in this House) whose brother is on HMS *Active* says his brother lately touched land (in Scotland) for the first time for *four weeks*. They had no bread all that time (for some reason not very clear).

It seems as if Turkey will join Germany, doesn't it? The general impression among military correspondents seems to be that the real war will begin when we get to the Rhine. At present we are said to be merely skirmishing. Of course if we can manage somehow to make some great guns, like those with which the Germans knocked Antwerp about, we might do it . . . but I suppose we certainly haven't got those at present.

. . . By the way, I played in my first housematch (at Rugger) yesterday. I 'sustained' a cut on the back of my head, for which, as it bled rather profusely, I had to go round to the san after tea. Simey clipped all the hair off and squirted it and put about forty different ointments on it and about six plasters, and told me to come and see him in the morning. I must look just as if I've got mange, but I can't see it. It doesn't hurt . . .

With love to all,
Louis.

School House
[Postmarked: 26 October 1914]

Dear all,

Last Thursday I played in a Bigside. That is a game in which the XV and the next best XV play a sort of pick up. Sometimes

Masters play, for instance, Mr Lockhart[43] played in this one. I played back as usual. Mr Lockhart was much pleased with me.

About my work. I can only say that things go on much as usual. What Mr Collins thinks of me, the following incident may be taken as showing something (or nothing). The other morning at the beginning of the lesson (he always wastes half the time by fooling about making ridiculous remarks), he came up to where I sit and stood looking at me. Then he said, 'What do you mean . . . you intoler – able ruffian . . . you intoler – able ruffian . . . what do you mean by getting full marks for your Horace this morning? . . . Eh? . . . It's all right lad . . . it's all right . . . you're settling down well now lad . . . you'll get along splendidly.'

This is the sort of ridiculous man we have to deal with in this class.

Hilaire Belloc came down and lectured to us on Wednesday about 'The Strategy of War'. He spoke with a brilliant clearness both of voice and exposition. He started straight off with no humming or hahing, and carried the subject right up to the moment when he said, 'and now I must go, or I shall lose my train', and walked away.

You cannot conceive of anything more extraordinary than his clearness and thoroughness, using long words sometimes but always so that there was no possible question as to what he meant. His main points were (i) that numbers, i.e. numerical superiority, *other things being equal*, were always the deciding factor in a campaign.

(ii) That the Germans were numerically superior at present, but perhaps in the middle of November the Allies will be equal in numbers to them. That Russia could go on increasing her army so that when the Germanic powers had reached their full numerical strength, and ditto the French, English and Belgians, the whole Allies would be very considerably greater than the Germans. *But* that this is to be remembered: *that numbers, other things being equal, at the decisive time and place*, were the deciding factor. This constituted generalship, to be superior *at the decisive time and place*.

He then showed us about the retreat from Mons, which was, he says, quite intended to be a retreat, only really it was a rout . . .

Goodbye,
Love from Louis.

96

Headmaster: Most satisfactory in all ways. The House is the better for him.
Tutor: Going on very well.

School House
[Postmarked: 1 November 1914]

Dear everyone,
. . . I am quite all right now and hope (sincerely) to be able to play again on Tuesday. I have had great fun the last two halfs refereeing and coaching some of the lower games as I could not play myself . . . Dr David had a daughter yesterday . . .

It appears uncomfortably clear that the war will take its time. A splendid Rugbeian has just been killed. Major Arthur Jex-Blake Percival[44] (son of a former head master, now a Bishop) D.S.O., who had been lately decorated with the Cross of the Legion of Honour by President P[oincare]. There are two pictures of him in the matron's room here, a splendid looking chap. In one of them he has a long line of medals across his great strapping chest. I was talking to the matron last night. She said, 'All his medals never made him proud'.

. . . There are fifty Belgian wounded in the san here, and a lot of Belgian refugees in the town. Extraordinary looking people; they look fairly at a loss.

Isn't it witty the way when no news is forthcoming from the front, a ship or two ships regularly get blown up or sunk or something so as to provide the anxious public with some news.

I believe I was fifth for the half, which might have been worse. I shall see if I can't be top this half anyway. I haven't seen my report. Mr Collins is still pretty cheerful. He has been here about thirty years and there are a good many fellows in the form whose fathers were in the same form with him (Mr Collins) in the same form room. I mean Mr Collins *taught* them, not was at the school with them. He himself was here at school in about 1860.[45]

I am with love,
Louis.
(though you might not think it)

School House
[Postmarked: 15 November 1914]

Dear all,
 . . . Mr Collins came out with one of his famed jests the other day, which has not been heard for some years. A fellow kept on blowing his nose while he (Mr Collins) was attempting to explain Edward III's reign to us. So the irritated Jackie Collins turned on the wretched fellow with, 'Let it drip lad, let it drip'. It was frightfully funny. He told me I was a 'turbulent democrat'. . . .

With love to all. Hoping that you will last out,
Louis.

School House
[Postmarked: 22 November 1914]

Dear all,
 . . . Mr Odgers,[46] who takes us for French, tells us rather a witty thing. You know the French for Austrians is les Autrichiens; well the French soldiers call their enemies (the Austrians and Germany) les Autrichiens and les Autrechiens (if you follow).

With love from
Louis.

School House
[Postmarked: 29 November 1914]

Dear everyone,
 . . . There's not long now before I come home (I hope), not that I don't like it here, but it will be nice to be home again.
 I have [had] an awful row with Jackie Collins, which I will proceed to tell you about. At present I have a perfectly shocking cold. I use about eight handkerchiefs a day. Well, the other morning during a lesson everyone was blowing their noses so much that Jackie, who was in a very unusual mood that morning as he is

98

usually very cheerful, said, 'I won't have you making such a noise. I'll turn anybody out who blows his nose again.'

Well, of course, in about ten minutes I was in a ghastly state, and remarked sotto voce to the man next to me that I had the dickens of a cold. At the same time I gave a sort of wheeze, which I needn't have done if I'd been allowed to blow my nose.

Jackie heard this somehow, and looked up and asked if I was feeling all right, but he addressed the remark to the boy in front of me, who seemed to wonder what was happening. Then Jackie suddenly said, 'I believe you're at the bottom of this, Stokes'. ('All this' being more or less nothing at all). 'I won't have it', he said. 'Dry up, go and sit out there in the middle of the room where I can see you.'

This I did, and then as everybody shrieked with laughter I (rather naturally) did so too. Jackie was wild; he said he had a good mind to take me up to the Headmaster, which made everybody shriek as it was obvious I had done practically nothing. Certainly nothing he need have got angry about. Then he said I must sit there for the rest of term and keep very quiet if I didn't want to get into trouble. It was very difficult to stop laughing, as it was such an absurd scene over nothing.

Everyone I met after that said, 'I hear you've got into a row with Jackie, how absurd!' Etc. 'Jackie's rows are always about nothing at all.' Etc, etc.

Next day I said my lines and did work as usual; Jackie was quite as usual, said 'good' to my lines, and at second lesson remarked that I could sit in my old seat again if I liked and nothing more has been said . . .

You remember I told you that Jackie had congratulated a man in the form on his father being mentioned in despatches . . . Well, the chap's father has been killed (died of wounds).

I am very sorry for the poor chap, who has gone home for a few days. Perhaps you noticed Major E.B. Steel[47] RAMC in Saturday's list. That's him. The boy first heard on Thursday, and went home then. On Friday morning at first lesson it was a *very hard* what you call *sweaty* lesson (Livy) so Jack said we should have to have some hard work at this . . . then suddenly he noticed that Steel was not there, so he says, 'Hallo, where's Steel?' Somebody says, 'Gone home Sir.' 'Hallo,' says Jack, 'no bad news I hope.' 'His father's been killed Sir' . . . 'Oh dear,' says Jack, 'Oh dear, that's like one in the wind . . . 'Oh dear! . . . Oh dear! . . . we can't do any Livy now . . . we must just get along with it the best we can.' So we didn't do much Livy that lesson . . .

Now goodbye, with love to all,
Louis.

END-OF-TERM REPORT ADVENT 1914
Headmaster: Doing very well. I am sorry for his misfortunes.
Tutor: A very good term.

School House
[Internal evidence: 24 January 1915]

Dear Dad,

What I am going to say in this letter I meant to say on Thursday morning or Wednesday evening but there was no good opportunity. Perhaps I can say it as well on paper.

It is, why should not I enlist in the Army? The first objection is obviously because I am not old enough. But Walter[48] says that they would take me . . . and a boy in our House, under age, went as a driver in the A.S.C., and as you said in a letter last term that if I had been of 'military age' you would have let me go . . .

Another reason that seems to me to be of weight is that I think it very improbable indeed that I shall get a scholarship at the 'varsity, and it seems to me a great opportunity of making myself more fit and capable for the future . . . At any rate I ask you to give my idea consideration and not toss it aside as being ignorant and not thought out. You may say, 'You have no idea what a hard life it is'. I think I have a very fair idea, but because it might be hard that surely is no reason why it should be rejected; rather the better for me.

Do not think either that I have been influenced into thinking I want to go to the war by Walter or Wheatcroft[49] or anyone else, (as you do sometimes tell me, without much consideration for my own ideals and hopes). I assure you . . . it is my own idea, and I am pretty sure it would be just the life I want, for a bit anyway. I hope at any rate you will give it a sympathetic consideration.

With love,
Louis.

School House
[Postmarked: 24 January 1915]

Dear all

. . .as I told you I am in the Twenty. A striking Master called Cole[50] takes it. He is called 'Beaky' on account of his hooked nose. He is fearfully interesting, for in all his lessons Greek or Latin or English, he stops to discuss ethics etc, the wisdom of various politics that were adopted by the persons who occur in our lessons etc., which is interesting.

I have got a nice den from which I can hear the owls hooting in the Close. There has been one out there just now. Also I am in a select House Society (!) composed of the top few persons in the House (including all the Sixth). There are about a dozen in it this term. You pay a subscription and go up every night and have good food.

There are a fair number of troops billeted here, mostly Scotch. King's Own Scottish Borderers.

Love Louis.

School House
[Internal evidence: 1 February 1915]

Dear all,

. . . I am in a topping Maths set, same as last term, with the strange master (Mr Donkin) I told you about; he is quite bucked with me. I quite enjoy Maths, as indeed I do French and all my work, though public schools and above all Rugby, are terribly full of tradition, which is all right in some ways, but is apt to be cramping. Still . . .

An amusing comment in Dad's letter about the Hd. Master of Eton . . . I don't know much about him except what I've heard from Porchester[51], which is not greatly to his favour. He is loathed at Eton, but it must be a dreadful post.

[Unsigned]

101

[Internal evidence: 28 February 1915]

Dear all,

. . . We don't go in to Chapel before breakfast, instead we have C.O. in houses and go in to first lesson at 7.45. It is quite nice because we have time to look over our work before first lesson. The idea is I believe that people have been getting colds so much that till it gets warmer this system is to be used.

I have suddenly been elected secretary of the School House Debating Society! I have been a member of this for rather over a year, though I have only been to one meeting of it and only two debates, at neither of which I spoke. But the secretary is not allowed to be a member of the Sixth, and so as all the other members have left – by a process of elimination – I as the senior member not in the Sixth have become secretary. I have to get up the debate, which is pretty funny, as I have never gone in for debates at all here. Nobody in their senses does.

However, it is rather funny and as nobody could think of a subject for debate, I shoved up a notice on the House board as follows: 'WHEREAS it is intended to hold a House Debate on Saturday March 6th next, only nobody can think of anything to debate about, suggestions for a suitable subject are sincerely solicited, and should be registered below in a legible hand.' Please note the magnificent 'sister Susie' alliteration, also the idiomatic 'whereas'. I composed this brilliant effort during Chapel.

Everybody is frightfully bucked with it and there are already about ten suggestions up: vivisection, ex-Housemasters, Is the House going to the dogs?, Does the public school education encourage pride, vainglory and hypocrisy?, etc.

Yesterday I ran for the School against Shrewsbury Running VIII. I just got bottom place in our VIII.

[Unsigned]

HALF-TERM REPORT LENT 1915
Headmaster: I think he realizes the peculiar responsibility which his position in the House imposes on him. He can't help leading. I do not like the drop of nine places. Making all allowance for unsettlement I am sure that he can do better than this.

Tutor: Having considerable force of character he is in a position of some influence in the House, but as he is rather wanting in ballast, that influence seems likely to be more hearty than inspiring.

School House
[Postmarked: 8 March 1915]

Dear all,

. . . It is disgraceful that we have not got a half for poor de Pass's[52] VC. Everybody is fearfully fed [up]. All other schools get halves when such remarkable things happen. Just like Rugby.

. . . We had a remarkable lecture from Seton Thompson on Thursday. I do wish you had been there. You would have been immensely pleased with it. He gave some remarkable wolf-calls. He speaks very well. Very American he is, beautifully built with great shoulders and loose strong limbs.

Nothing more to say except
love from Louis.

P.S.   No comment is made by any of you on the fact that I ran for the school against Shrewsbury, which [is] the great running event of the year, and running is the great thing at Rugby after rugger and cricket. Perhaps it was because I came in last, but as I explained I was in my CO place.

The debate came off yesterday that 'This House considers that the Public Schools encourage pride, vainglory and hypocrisy'. I think they do, but spoke with Bateson[53] against. We won by twenty votes; raised a laugh or two, the main point.

School House
[Undated: mid-March 1915]

Dear all

. . . By the way, will Dad please just mention that he gives me leave to go in for the 'Crick' Run. This is a famous Rugby institution which takes place once a year, and you have to get leave from home to go in it as it is supposed to be rather far – thirteen miles. But I have already been round the course. I went on

Thursday with two masters, Odgers and Raven, and two boys. We got caught in the snowstorm six miles from home along a straight road with the snow blowing straight in our faces. Horribly cold; we just had to run on. Dreadful it was.

. . . The boy who was head of the House for my first year, W.H. Clarke, was killed at St Eloi last week. His brother had already been killed at the Aisne. His father[54] is in command of a Division . . . Horrible I think the war is.

Love Louis.

School House
[Postmarked: 22 March 1915]

My dear Dad,

I write in answer to your letter in which you ask (very reasonably) what I have to say about my report, before you make any comment on it.

I must go back to the beginning of the term to get to the bottom of this. When I received your letter saying that you could not think of my going to the War, I was (reasonably or unreasonably) extraordinarily sick about it; and all the more so because the arguments you used were just those – the old ones – I had expected, and which I could not believe were convincing. There was the one about not being old enough; well it seemed to me that if Arthur senior went, why shouldn't I? And besides I thought they wouldn't bother much about my age.

But the one that made me most bitter at the time, the bitterness is past, was that which avowed I was not strong enough.

I should like to say a few things on this point, because if I say plainly and without attempt to be scathing or anything (which I felt inclined to after your letter) it may help to smooth matters.

It has always seemed to be your's and mother's policy to not let us *strain* ourselves. That has seemed to run through all our upbringing. It is absurd of course to deny the wiseness of the motive. But when it is carried to such a pitch that you objected, if you remember, once to my riding to Newmarket on a bike to stay with Vaile; and you objected again to my walking to Wallingham. This (rightly or wrongly) riled me intensely . . .

Well, the thing is that here I have a reputation for being strong. A master, Mr Raven, said to a boy here who told it to me, 'Stokes is very strong'. I am back for my House, and though I have not played for the School at Rugger, I have played among the 1st thirty players last season. I have run for the School. I have run three years in the House Relay Team, (I am the only member left who ran three years ago). I am in my House XI – Mr H.C. Bradby wanted me to play at Lords against Marlborough. Boxing – when I hoped to attain some skill at it, you stopped me. There is only one fellow in the School now besides me who was in each Cock House team last year.

This eulogy is all entirely with the view of showing you that here I am looked upon as strong. Your standards must be different. I have not topped out at *all* (except for my accident) for two whole years.

Well, you of course have your point of view, that riled me very much. I felt (and feel), I am thankful to say, perfectly fit and well and to have it from time to time suggested to me that I am delicate is not, however true it may be, supposing it is, to be expected to make one pleasant on the subject.

Well, after that I can tell you my work rocked a bit. I believe I tried honestly enough at it while I was doing it, but I grew rather reckless. And here I should say that what you said about being very disappointed if I didn't get a scholarship made me all the more rocking, as it seemed – and seems – so very, very unlikely that I shall get one. Just the very day that letter of yours came we were doing the ode of Horace which starts:

'Angustam amice pauperiem pati
robustus acri militia puer condiscat . . .'

and our form-master laid stress on the fact that it is not, 'let the boy learn to become strong by bearing the hard stresses etc'. You can see how that did for me. The ode goes on to say, 'vitamque sub divo et trepidis agat in rebus'. 'And let him live a life out of doors and in dangerous things'. And a few lines later the famous, 'dulce et decorum est pro patria mori'. I have tried to show you my point of view. I am trying to be sympathetic with yours, because I think without sympathy we might as well give it up. You will see that I am fearfully bucked with everything, enjoying every moment of life here and at home; trying, I do hope, to be kind and courageous if nothing else. And so when, what mind you *seemed to me*, little, petty, unsympathetic, restraining influences and arguments came in, I was upset and as I say rocked.

Well Dr David had me up after about a fortnight of term and said he wasn't very satisfied with my work. I told him I was sick because it seemed I would not be allowed to go to the War.

He said he could quite understand that, but he seemed to be sorry that I had got upset by it. He said, 'You know you mustn't let your feelings carry you away like that . . . Besides your father's let you be in the Corps, as it is.' Which is true, and which I am very grateful for.

Then I told him how I wanted to go to the War. He said that of course I did. He said, 'Of course you are quite strong enough and all that'. (I think there are only three other boys in this House of eighty-five who have a cold bath besides me every day.) But he said he didn't think unless I gave a wrong age I should have a dog's chance of getting out to the War. I told him I should like to drive in the A.S.C. or Artillery, as a boy in our House is doing (who was not by any means strong as you would call it). He told me this boy is not allowed out yet though he is eighteen, and he said he really didn't think I should get out if I tried. Well there you have why my work was 'uneven'. I have told the tale, it can speak for itself. I don't want to excuse it, or anything else in my past career over which we have had painful scenes. I only wish that we had more sympathy betweeen us. I believe we shall do . . . I think I have been doing all right this half, but I am no classic at heart, and that's the touble. If, like you, I was a *scholar* and held learning and books first or at any rate essential, it would be different. But, though I like everything I am not *mad* on Classics etc.

Well, this is a long letter. The point of it is meant to be to clear away all the rotten doubt and misunderstanding there has been; *to own, without reservation, that I have been often wrong*, and probably shall be again, but to assure you sincerely that my heart is high and my hopes are happy, my head is clear and my hand (a good sign) strong and to beg for sympathy which is needed.

With love from Louis.

Dear Dad,

Thank you for letter, which gave me great satifaction.

I don't want to argue or object to anything you say in your letter, because as I say it gave me great pleasure, and was very fair to me. I don't know if you have ever read Stevenson's 'Apology for Idlers'. That says, better than I can, my case; namely that what may seem idling to some is to others a joy.

Still, as I say, I don't want to pick holes. I'd rather fall in with your ideas. So next holidays, for an hour or so, you will see your desire. I cannot honestly say I view this prospect with delight, because I like to read when the spirit moves me, but still it shall be done.

Again thanking you for your letter.

Love from Louis.

School House
[Postmarked: 31 March 1915]

Dear all

. . . I told you there were Scotch soldiers here; fine specimens with a distinct difference, of course, to the Welsh lads.

There were a good many officers billeted here. One of them, so a lad in the House tells me, remarked to him that, 'this is a fine School'.

You hear Annie Laurie a good deal, whistled and on the bagpipes.

A wounded officer of the K[ing's] O[wn] Scottish Borderers (Amos' regiment you remember) told a boy here that the regiment has been cut up.

Another boy whose father is in the Indian Army says a lot of the Indian soldiers have been sent home because nearly all their officers have been killed, and you can't put an ordinary English officer in an Indian regiment, so they have gone back. Also they felt the cold to a much worse degree than our men did.

It is very nice where I sit at meals now having a *loaf* of bread which one can cut oneself, instead of – as the majority of people have to – having bits of bread already cut, as often as not (when there is not new bread) picked up off the floor by the boys who serve at table, and shoved into the bread baskets . . .

Love to all,
Louis.

School House
[Postmarked: 4 April 1915]

My dears,

. . . In spite of my constitutional (and very regrettable) delicacy, I have managed (where but a bare dozen or so in the House have done) to keep in School all this term; and that in an Easter term that has been, if anything, worse than the ordinary for colds etc. There have been at times ten out of twenty-five stopping out in our form . . .

. . . Dreadful to see so many killed. We had a memorial service this afternoon to those O.R.s who have been killed since the last one (in November). Their names were read out; a long list. We have had about seventy killed altogether. One was called G. de M. Armstrong-Lushington-Tulloch[55]. A mouthful!

With love to all,
Louis.

END-OF-TERM REPORT LENT 1915
Headmaster: He is in turmoil. His originality, independence and strong vitality have been leading him, and possibly others, astray a little. Presently he will realize that there is good reason behind our methods of House government and other traditions. I believe him to be perfectly sound in essentials. The work report is a great improvement.
Tutor: Seems to be discontented for no good reason. He would do well to remember that to be much in evidence, unless perhaps being useful, is always bad.

School House
[Postmarked: 9 May 1915]

Dear all,

Here I am again in the same form, den, dormitory, House, School, etc. Consequently, there is little news to send you.

Four boys in yesterday's 'wounded' were here with me; two in the House. I expect you noticed Poulton's death; he came from this House, you may remember.

The Scotch troops who were billeted here last term have been in action with the Mediterranean force and badly cut up. The officer the Bradbys had billeted on them has been wounded.

from Louis.

School House
[Internal evidence: 16 May 1915]

Dear all,

Great excitement here the last two days. Within a dozen yards of the School House, down the High Street, there is a barber's and post office combined, held by a German, Meerholz by name. On Friday night as we were going to bed, the butler (Mr Busby) brought news that a crowd was collecting round the unfortunate man's shop. They could be seen from certain dormitory windows. Just as ten o'clock struck (at which silence, 'lights-out', begins to reign in the dormitory), a roar from the crowd was heard, and for the next hour we were treated – in Rugby – to the shouts of a mob. Every now and then one could hear the voice of a speaker, it seemed, urging them, and then a roar would go up, cries and hoots, and the speaker waxed more intensive (they say the old man godlike David went out to them) . . . I think nobody but myself heard the actual bricks being thrown; certainly nobody I asked in the morning heard them . . . few but I were awake, when crash! Followed by a burst of cheering. About five minutes later another crash! as of brick on glass . . . In the morning the window of Meerholz Hairdresser was seen, at least what was left of it, to be smashed in two places. After a bit it was all boarded up. Meerholz himself was arrested I believe. This was not all. At Long Lawford, about two miles away, there lives a gentleman father of a boy in the school (G.F. Bradby's house), who has been a naturalized Englishman or German (if you follow) for forty-three years. He came to England because he disapproved of Bismarck's 'blood and iron'. He was a J.P. though he resigned at the beginning of the war because a prisoner objected to being tried by him.

Well, rumours went about that his house was to be raided at night (last night) by the Rugby mob. At six o'clock walking out via the old quad into the Close, I was mildly surprised to see a posse (is this the word?) of policemen, about nine of them, sitting and standing about in the quad. Later, about seven o'clock, practically the whole population of Rugby was to be seen coming up the High Street and turning and walking towards Long Lawford; hundreds and hundreds of them. I haven't heard if anything happened, but apparently there is still a row, as a lot of bobbies were sitting in Old Big School this afternoon, so it has been rather moving.[56]

Several people lately who were here with me, in the lists. Vincent[57] – killed; he used to be in the same Maths set with me, and throw me chocolate from the back, (I sat in front). Hoyle – killed; who was head of football in this house last year (1913–1914). J.C.D. Brown[58], who was in the House with me – killed. J.T. Bretherton, also in the House with me (his brother[59] is here now) – wounded; shot right through the body *at point blank range*. C.P. Johnstone[60], the great Johnstone, who got his XI, whom I was in the same form with . . . he was always very decent to me – wounded very badly. A bullet went through his face, neck and into his lung (same bullet). Benham[61], in the School with me – killed. Hodgson[62], in the House with me – wounded. Fyfe-Jamieson[63], wounded again; in the school with me. Do you see, I know quite a lot of it . . . Also Vertue[64] – killed; in the school with me. I once got him a dreadul knock in the mouth bowling against him in a game. He got the Medaille Militaire. This is a sad list, and mine only! . . .

[I] send you all, love.
Goodbye from
Louis.

School House
[Internal evidence: mid-May 1915]

Dear Dad,

Many happy returns of the day! I hope you will have a happy birthday; thank you for your letter.

I shall do all I can (by Grace Divine) to get a scholarship, and need hardly say I hope I shall. Dr David suggested Corpus to me as a likely college. I think it would be very pleasing to get one there.

with love from
Louis.

School House
[Postmarked: 23 May 1915]

Dear all,

. . . Have been walking in David's two gardens, which he opens to School House people on Sunday evenings. They are lovely, with lilac, bluebells etc out, as I suppose they must be at home.

Sam Attenborough's brother[65] . . . has died of wounds this week. He was in the Canadians, Winnipeg Regiment. Sam's den is next door, we go about together a good deal. All his brothers (5) are serving, and he goes to Sandhurst next term. Another Rugby boy here last year and Captain of the XI[66] has probably been killed; when last heard of he was in a trench that had been mined . . .

Love to all,
Louis.

P.S. The marmalade is very good. I suppose Grannie must be better.

School House
[Postmarked: 31 May 1915]

Dear all

. . . The War is dreadful isn't it? We don't seem to get much forwarder either . . . Hilaire Belloc comes to give us his views on the war soon . . .

Yesterday the House Mission Boys from Notting Hill came for their annual visit, and there was the annual meeting in the Speechroom in the evening. There was not nearly so many boys this year of course, as lots have gone to the war. Thirty odd have been killed. A club boy is Smith-Dorrien's orderly; another club boy got the D.C.M. This boy is reported, after walking about seventeen miles in snow and rain and then waiting an hour or two in the rain before attacking, to have said, 'Well, thank Gawd there ain't no wasps'!

. . . Over one hundred O.R.s have been killed up to date, 142 wounded. The boy whose prayer book I use in Chapel and who was here in the House last summer has been wounded by gas, but is 'going on well'. There is a picture in last week's 'London News' of the fat officer of the Seaforths, Macdougall who left last year. He was an awful sportsman.

Love to all,
Louis.

HALF-TERM REPORT TRINITY 1915
Headmaster: I am well pleased. He is showing his best. (He has just renounced farm labour for school work.)
Tutor: There has been a considerable improvement this term in his attitude to things in general and he is giving much more satisfaction.

School House
[Postmarked: 13 June 1915]

Dear all
. . . On Wednesday Belloc came and gave his lecture. He really was splendid; better than any of his three others I have heard – all brilliant as they were. I would rather hear him than anyone I think. His main points were as follows:

1. Now, and for the next five or six weeks we are at the crisis of the War. That is, after the next five or six weeks there will be no doubt as to the result of the war, however long it may take.

2. What are we fighting for? In the first phase of the War we were fighting to prevent Germany being all powerful in Europe.

After the Battle of the Marne that fear was finally disposed of. Now we are fighting to prevent Germany being at all powerful in Europe and correspondingly the Germans are fighting to maintain their power as a nation. This is the danger of what may happen. The Germans may say, we don't want Belgium, and leave it, all except Antwerp which we should like as a sea base. They might even give up Alsace Lorraine, or part of it, and Poland. Then the War will change again and we shall be fighting not for anything but to exterminate Germany. The Germans see these possibilities, and it may be very hard and very long before we can fix them properly.

3. The Germans are definitely, in men and munitions and trade and food, *inferior to the allies*. Their only hope lies in the fact that that inferiority is unevenly distributed and on the west and south they are superior in *available* material to the allies. *They know this.* They *know* they can't break through in the west, because *other things being equal numbers* win in war. *So* it is vital for them to break out on the east, and this is what they are now trying to do in their great assault in Galicia and at the Dneister. If they can pierce the Russian line here, *we may not be able* to beat them for three years.

4. If we can free the Dardanelles, we can equip millions more Russians. But he regards the Dardanelles as next door to impossible to force.

5. *The great card* is the Anglo-French offensive. *If that succeeds*, the Germans will be beat and they know it. If it does not quite succeed, it will have been a ghastly waste of money, men and munitions, because the Germans will still be able to stay in the west – with the odds slightly against us. And he said if one can give any advice to an audience of boys, then remember if this offensive *just* fails to be completely successful, then more than ever we must determine to see the thing through. The talk about our being short of munitions, he said, is 'Harmsworth talk'!! We are making five-sixths of our maximum possible output. We are immensely superior to the Germans in ammunition . . .

Love to all,
Louis.

Dear all,

. . . Did you see the pictures of the fellows hoeing etc? I believe there was one in the 'Daily News'. It was amusing in one paper to see the heading 'Rugby boys exchange play for work'!!!! As a matter of fact you get off not only preparation the night before you go (as you don't go in to first lesson), but also preparation when you come in in the evening, because you are supposed to be too tired, although you arrive home at 5.30. A boy played a most strenuous game of squash rackets with me after working in the fields the other evening . . .[67]

A man called Pollen[68] comes this week to lecture to us about the Navy. He's the man who writes in 'Land & Water', instead of Fred Jane who used to, but wasn't thought much of I think . . .

Poulton left one of his motors in his will to Mr Evers, a School House tutor I may have mentioned to you, who was a great friend of his. A picture of Poulton's grave hangs under the cloister by the far side of the School House door . . .

The boy who sits on the other side of me at meals doesn't sit there any longer, because he was offered a commission in a Lancashire Brigade of Artillery about four weeks ago, and left. Also the boy who sat next me at maths left yesterday to take a commission in the Sherwood Foresters

Nothing of interest to tell you,
so love to you all from
Louis.

School House
[Postmarked: 5 July 1915]

Dear everyone,

. . . We had a very fine lecture on Thursday by Mr Pollen 'the naval expert'. He told us about how big guns are aimed; it was very interesting. He explained the remarkable difficulties in the way of accurate shooting . . .

. . . On Tuesday the Corps is to be inspected by some Colonel; the man who inspected us two years ago had died of wounds.[69] On

Saturday we have an all-day field day, I think, with two other schools – The Oratory School (where Belloc was) and Warwick Grammar School, or something else.[70]

Did you see Dr Jex-Blake[71] has died. He was the only O.R. Head Master for years and years. By the way one of the teeth Mr Rhodes stopped (right hand side upper storey) has come unstopped . . .

I am a Lance Corporal in the Corps, which I have mentioned before I think, but I do so again as an excuse for adding that (not being in the Guards!) I wear one stripe on either arm . . .

Nothing more, this is long enough already
love to all,
Louis.

School House,
[Postmarked: 12 July 1915]

Dear all,

. . . The boy I told you I fagged for three summers ago who was mentioned in despatches has got the Military Cross. 'July 3. Sec. Lieut. Henry Morrant Stanford, 32nd Bat RFA. For consistently gallant conduct both at Neuve Chapelle and again on May 9, 1915, during operations near Rouges Bancs, in keeping up communication by mending telephone lines under heavy fire. He has done excellent work as Observing Officer for the last six months, and the accuracy of the wirecutting by the 32nd Battery Royal Field Artillery, on May 9 was due to his precise observations.'[72]

All the five boys I fagged for all have got commissions. One has been killed, one severely wounded, and one the Military Cross. The wounded one I fagged for in my first term in the House, he had some very nice little hyacinth bulbs which he instructed me to water. I did this very heartily; and my heartiness increased as I saw they were not growing. In fact they were beginning to turn brownish. One day their owner came to my den and said, 'Oh, Stokes, I don't think you need water my hyacinths any more thanks.' I had drowned them, but he gave me two cakes at the end of term.

. . . Most of my friends of *my term* are leaving this term (who have not already) and importune me for a photograph. So unless I

115

hear from Dad to the contrary on Thursday, I will take the liberty of getting a photo taken. *I must pay for this myself*, as it is entirely my affair.

Nothing of interest to tell you
so love to you all,
Louis.

School House
[Postmarked: 20 July 1915]

Dear Mother & Dad,

. . . I was fearfully bucked with these presents and had a topping birthday. A boy Clayton, who was in Bullocks with me and in S.H. and who left today to go in the Navy, bought me some marmalade. Chris Bullock[73] has been wounded in the thigh in France. He is now in London, going on nicely . . .

. . . Wheatcroft sent me some scholarship papers to look at. They seem very hard, but still it won't hurt me I suppose to have a try, though I *wonder* if it is worth my while. Lockhart who has just been in with my report, says he thinks it is, but I don't know what he knows about it. Still I must talk to you on the subject when I get home . . .

Love Louis.

School House
[Internal evidence: 25 July 1915]

Dear All,

. . .We go to camp on Wednesday July 26th, and return all being well on Friday Aug 6th to Rugby, whence I hope to come straight on home and arrive on the usual train the same day . . .

Our camp address is

Rugby OTC Camp
Fawsley
Charwellton
Nr Daventry

It is a large manor house that we are going to be at, not in tents as I suppose the difficulty of getting them is too great. There are lots of topping things there and it ought to be no end of a lark.

116

Each platoon provides twelve men to act one night as a guard, that is sentries round the house. It ought to be rather fun. We go on duty the first night there. We are marching to camp.

The sentries not actually doing sentry duty may go to sleep, but the corporal of the guard must wake up every two hours to take the reliefs out, and once a night the whole guard has to turn out and be inspected when the officer of the day comes round and inspects them. The officer of the day comes round firstly soon after lights out and clanks his sword to let you know he's coming. The sentry near the guard tent then says 'Halt'; if he halts, 'who goes there', 'visiting rounds'; then the sentry shouts 'turn out guard' till someone in the guard wakes up. We have all sorts of instructions as to what to do with suspicious characters, and all together it ought to be great fun . . .

I wonder if Dad could procure me some books for reading up in the hols. I have been studying the schol. papers Wheatcroft sent me, and they look to me rather hard, . . . still I can have a good try. What I must do is get a clear idea of the most important things in Greek, Roman, and English History as far as I can see from these papers. So could Dad get from the Library the best books for me to read on these subjects? I don't want deeply scientific historical studies. I want to know what happened and why sort of thing, who Pericles was and what he did, which I always forget. Then some book on literature because they always ask questions comparing literatures of different periods; then I must read from Homer and Cicero, and do a few proses and generally try to get a sound footing in such things. It ought to be interesting anyhow, whatever the results, which I must say I view with grave doubt . . .

> Well, so long,
> Love,
> Louis.

[Internal evidence: 29 July 1915]
[Written on Rugby OTC headed paper]

Dear all,

. . . It is *awful sport* here [at Fawsley]; huge, big, splendid house, with courtyards and things and clocks, and a vast park going for miles like at Childerditch, plenty of lakes and things. We, the S.H. platoon, have the library, a big room to ourselves. I will describe the day. Reveille 6.00 a.m., get up and bathe if you like. Dress, clean your buttons, and arrange your kit and fall in on parade. 7.00–8.00 drill. 8.15 breakfast. 9.30 inspection of kit, this has to be awful neat. 10.00–1.30 field work. 1.45 dinner. 4.00 parade, and rifles and bayonets inspected. 6.45 tea. 7.45 guard mounted and retreat sounded. 8.45 first post sounded. 9.00 last post sounded. 9.15 lights out.

All the odd times are filled up by bathing, playing golf with a tennis ball and a stick, playing football and whatnot, cleaning rifles, etc., etc., etc., etc. . . .

Love to all,
Louis.

END-OF-TERM REPORT TRINITY 1915
Headmaster: Good. He is giving what we ask, and is beginning to understand why we ask it. I am well satisfied.
Tutor: The best term he has had for some time. He has been taking things more seriously and making himself useful in the affairs of the House. He is also I think making an effort – a difficult one for him – towards appreciating points of view which do not coincide with his own.

School House
[Postmarked: 26 September 1915]

Dear all
 . . . The chief news is that I am in the Sixth which I suppose is nice to be in before you leave. I got in (luckily I must say) bottom but one. I am in charge of the biggest but one dormitory in the House. There are about fourteen boys in it, including Iles,[74] who sleeps next me and whom I talk to about Wolverhampton . . . I collected in Chapel today, but don't read the lesson till the last Sunday but one. I wear a white straw hat with a black ribbon round it to show who I am. Mr Kittermaster[75] is my form master.

Everyone seems pretty well here. A master called Wilson[76] (no relation) has just been killed at the front. He was an *awful* sort. He enlisted as a private but got a commission later.

I have got another den, not such a nice one, but the Sixth have to take what they are given as there has to be a Sixth in each passage. This one looks out on to the quad. It is the one I used to clean out when I was fag to that boy (two years ago) whom I told you had got the Military Cross 'for consistent gallantry for 6 months'. I have got three fags (if you please). I got here with all my luggage well in hand for once, and everything I want seems to have been packed very well . . .

By the way the two bottom members of the Sixth in the House have to run the House Bank. So on Friday night I and the lad who got into the Sixth in this House besides me, trotted round the House collecting money. We got about £73 and 9 rupees! This last from the Thibetan boy (at least one of the Thibetan boys – there are two in the House now).

With love to all
from
Louis

School House
[Postmarked: 3 October 1915]

Dear all,

. . . It has turned much colder since I left you. In fact the cold days seem to have set in at last for good.

Simultaneously with this natural process a splendid rule has been made by the Head of this House that everyone in the House is to have a cold bath before first lesson in the mornings. This is a very sound rule as there is nothing so healthy. But it is a blow I fancy to some old frowsters; and is far from being a popular rule . . . The rule does not make any difference to me as I always did have one . . .

In these late long lists of officers there have been several Rugby names, three of boys who were here with me (one has two brothers now in the school). One of these boys was in the Sixth little more than a year ago. Mr Cawley[77] was a Rugby boy . . . That poem on the war by the head of Shrewsbury[78] has disappeared from the quad, so I cannot send a copy, but I may meet it somewhere about. The other Sixth in my dorm who came back last night saw one of the Zeppelins over London, 'a great long yellow thing', a good way off with anti-aircraft shells bursting below it.

love to all,
Louis.

P.S.   A brother of Mr Lockhart has just been killed.

School House
[Postmarked: 17 October 1915]

Dear all,

. . . A few more Rugby boys killed. The boy who has carved his name on the desk I sit at, most prominent among them. Also J. O. Iles[79] whom I have told you of. He was a Sixth in the House [in] my first year. He swam and played chess for Cambridge. A cousin of the Iles here now . . .

Do you remember a Mr Bailey at the Red House Inn, or some such inn at Cransford? If you do he had a son who was recently gas poisoned at the front. A dreadful thirst was brought on by this and he drank some water from a stream which the Germans had put some arsenic in. Bad luck, and is now in England dying. He is said not to be able to live long . . .

Love Louis.

School House
[Postmarked: 24 October 1915]

Dear all,

. . . We had a good sermon by a preacher called Ward[80] today. The text was, 'stand up and build . . . so they strengthened their hand to the work', or something like that.

He pointed out the great task there was before the young of this generation who, though probably most of them would not have to fight upon the fields of Flanders, would have their part in perhaps five or ten years in *justifying the war* by living actually in life and fact, all the truths and best things in religion that we have known all along, and for which we are not fighting . . .

I had a long letter from Walter this week. He seems cheerful. He is in a machine gun section now and has an anti-aircraft gun which he dashes out with when an aeroplane is sighted, has a shot, and hares back again before they can drop a shell on him. The other day he said a mess was blown to pieces by a shell within a few yards of him. He had to carry away what was left. He would like you to write to him I'm sure sometimes . . .

Love to all,
Louis.

HALF-TERM REPORT ADVENT 1915

Headmaster: Most valuable. I only wish that he might stay to help us longer, but I recognize the higher call. He has worked well and bravely, and the place is most creditable.
Tutor: He has taken most kindly to his new position of responsibility and is setting an excellent example of vigorous enthusiasm.

School House
[Postmarked: 1 November 1915]

Dear all,
. . . We had a memorial service yesterday for the boys killed between now and June 20th. Many names. It was sad to see the sad fathers and mothers. In this week's 'Illustrated News' in the right hand bottom corner of the page of killed officers you will see three Rugby boys together, all here with me. Inglis[81], Wolley Dod[82] and Iles, the last two in S.H.

Love to all from
Louis.

School House
[Postmarked: 14 November 1915]

Dear all
. . . On Tuesday we had a field day with Harrow against Eton. It was at a place called Wendover, thirty miles due east of Oxford.
It poured with rain during the whole operation which added to the fun . . . I attached myself to a Harrow section (by mistake) with whom I stayed for almost twenty mins. They pointed me out their headmaster, who was down watching. Later we had a great rout of the Eton boys on a great beechwood ridge. I caught hold of an Eton corporal and pulled him to earth, informing him he was my prisoner. Which, though at first he stoutly denied it, he later

admitted when he saw I had fairly got hold of him. Just at this triumphant moment, however, two other Eton boys burst from the wood beind, fell over us and on top of us and proclaimed me their prisoner. There was a wild scene in which they demanded my ammunition and I told them with some warmth what they were if they couldn't see I had a dummy rifle and so on, when suddenly 'cease fire' blew and we dispersed, but I found a great piece of the coporal's mackintosh that I had torn off, on the ground. I carried this proudly off, and it is now our section mascot, and is to have the names of the section inscribed on it, and handed down to the members of the section as one after the other leave.

It was grand fun, and so it was to get hot tea afterwards.

. . . Nothing else to report except that I went to Oundle yesterday, as back for the 2nd XV. Had a good time, they are a decent lot of fellows and rather a decent school. Also I have got my 'bags', which is a football distinction here which allows you to wear black stockings and your House crest in front of your hat. In my case a black skull and crossbones on a red ground. To save expense of getting black stockings, haven't I some at home you could send? Also you might send 7/6 which was the journey money to Oundle and which I had to borrow from a boy. Nothing more.

Love to all,
Louis.

P.S. . . . I enclose a poem of Rupert Brooke's for Margaret, which I think is good and may please her. I should like to hear what you think of it.

School House
[Postmarked: 22 November 1915]

Dear all

. . . Things go on. The weather is still very fine (is it St Luke's summer or something?), though in the early mornings and the evenings and at all times by the yellow leaves on the trees you can see that it is autumn.

Every week more boys I know are killed or wounded. In this week's 'Illustrated London News', you will see a fine picture of a splendid boy who left only a year ago from this House, Lieut D. K. Wolley-Dod. His Colonel wrote of his coolness in difficult

122

positions and how he was setting a splendid example of cheerfulness in a big bombardment of our trenches when he was killed instantly by a shell.

. . . An Old Rugbeian who was a signalman in the R.N.V.R. and was captured on the retreat from Antwerp, lately escaped from his prison in Germany. [He] walked 180 miles (by night, hiding in woods in the day; he passed as a German workman) to the coast of Denmark. He walked along the coast until he found a boat and rowed half-way to England in it (eleven miles) when he was picked up by a Danish picket boat and taken to Denmark. There he was kept 'in quarantine' for a bit and later sent to England! . . .

Love to all,
Louis.

School House
[Postmarked: 30 November 1915]

My dear everyone

. . . How shocking it will be if the Suffragettes make any disturbance in Church! I am indeed glad that I am not at home to witness such lawless scenes. I really shouldn't quite know what to do about it.

There is a confirmation here tomorrow, because so many people got measles last Easter and so couldn't be confirmed then. Everybody attends; it is a very dull service, I think, if you are not taking an active part in it. Especially if (as there was the only time I have watched it) there is a huge pillar blocking all view of the Bishop.

. . . Exams for us start on Dec 13th which I am looking forward to; they are more interesting in many ways than ordinary work . . .

Yours with love,
Louis.

School House
[Postmarked: 5 December 1915]

Dear all,

I told Dr David I should like to go in the Marines, so he wrote to the Admiralty and got the necessary papers and has filled them in and written me a recommendation which he says he will send them if you agree.

So I send you the printed paper the Admiralty sent, so that you can see.

I like the idea of the Marines because they go on the sea; that is my reason for wanting to join them. Dr David has written . . . for my Corpus papers. I mean entrance or application papers or whatever they are called. I think the exam starts on Tuesday week and Dr David is letting us come home on Saturday, so I expect I shall do that, but I will let you know during the week.   I can't say I think I shall get a scholarship, for I don't think I am good enough, and I am not hopeful. But if I don't I might try after the war. I should like to.

Love from Louis.

NOTES TO PART TWO

1   Lt-Col H.J. Harris, *A History of the First Hundred Years of the Rugby School Corps, 1860–1960* (n.d.) p.59.
2   Ibid.
3   Collis, *Silver Fleece*, p.35.
4   Ibid.
5   *Meteor*, 580, 21 December, 1914.
6   Parker, *The Old Lie*, p.17.
7   Ibid., p.18.
8   E. Raymond, *Tell England* (1922), p.168.
9   William Chawner Brooke (Brooke's 1901–6): served in the Royal Naval Division; died aboard ship in the Aegean Sea, 23 April, 1915.
10 'Peace', quoted in B. Gardner (Ed.), *Up the Line to Death, The War Poets 1914–1918* (1976), p.10.
11 *Meteor*, 580, 21 December, 1914.
12 *Meteor*, 577, 15 October, 1914.
13 Harris, *Rugby School Corps*, p.59.
14 Ibid., p.12. For Louis' description of this event see his letter of 17 July, 1912 as above pp.49–50.
15 Ibid., pp.31–2.
16 Quoted in Parker, *The Old Lie*, p.64.
17 Harris, *Rugby School Corps*, p.58.
18 Simpson, *Schoolmaster's Harvest*, p.68.
19 G. Huxley, *Both Hands* (1970), p.51.
20 Collis, *Silver Fleece*, p.35.
21 Harris, *Rugby School Corps*, p.68.
22 *Meteor*, 579, 27 November, 1914.
23 Parker, *The Old Lie*, p.34.
24 Huxley, *Both Hands*, p.46.
25 Quoted in Parker, *The Old Lie*, p.68.
26 P.F. Alexander, *William Plomer; A Biography* (1990), p.33.
27 Donald William Akers Hankey (Collins' 1898–1901): served with 7th Bn Rifle Brigade and 3rd Bn Royal Warwickshire Regt; killed on the Somme, 12 October, 1916.

28   D. Hankey, *A Student in Arms* (1917), pp.59–64.

29   In September, 1993, there were seventy-eight full-time members of staff and 669 pupils; a staff/pupil ratio of 8.6, compared to a ratio of 15.4 in 1914.

30   Collis, *Silver Fleece*, p.35.

31   Hugh Stanley Wilson, appointed as an assistant master in 1911; served with 8th Bn Worcester Regt; killed at Hebuterne on 14 September, 1915. Hubert Podmore, appointed as an assistant master in 1910; served with 6th Bn Northamptonshire Regt; accidentally killed in Flanders on 31 December, 1917. Oswald Massey Samson, appointed as an assistant master in 1903; served with RGA; died of wounds in northern France on 17 September, 1918.

32   Collis, *Silver Fleece*, p.52.

33   Ibid., p.55.

34   A. Waugh, *Loom of Youth* (1917), p.36. This novel caused a storm on publication because it was critical of the public school system, at the very time that the schools were thought to be proving themselves and vindicating their ethos.

35   Quoted in Parker, *The Old Lie*, p.271.

36   Ibid.

37   Collis, *Silver Fleece*, p.66.

38   One Old Rugbeian called the first chapter of his war memoirs 'The new school'; see J. Nettleton, *The Anger of Guns* (1979).

39   John [Jack] Collins was appointed as an assistant master in 1875 and died in 1916 while still teaching at the school.

40   Edward Fenwick Boyd (Wilson's 1904–9): served with 1st Bn Northumberland Fusiliers; mentioned in despatches; killed at Vailly on 20 September, 1914.

41   Arthur Octavian Boyd (SH 1895–8): served with RFA; mentioned in despatches twice.

42   Lord Porchester, Henry George Alfred Marius Victor Francis Herbert (SH 1913–15): served with 7th Hussars.

43   J. H. B. Lockhart served with Seaforth Highlanders, and later the Intelligence Corps attached to the RFC; housemaster 1923–1930.

44   Arthur Jex-Blake Percival (SH 1887–8): served with Northumberland Fusiliers; awarded Legion of Honour, DSO, mentioned in despatches twice; killed in France on 31 October, 1914.

45   Collins was a pupil in Rugby School from 1863–7.

46   Francis William Odgers, appointed as an assistant master in 1911; served as a housemaster from 1920–35.

47   Edwin Bedford Steel (Morice's 1886–9): served with Royal Army Medical Corps, 1st Cavalry Division; mentioned in despatches; died of wounds on 23 November, 1914. His son, Anthony

Bedford Steel (Wilson's 1913–18), later served in the Army Service Corps.

48 Pte Walter O. Clarke, 10th Bn Royal Fusiliers.

49 Edward Louis Elam Wheatcroft was at Oundle School from 1911–15, and had attended St Faith's Preparatory School with Louis. Wheatcroft's father, Dr W.H. Wheatcroft, was a friend of Rev Henry Stokes and assisted Louis with his application to Corpus Christi, Cambridge.

50 Edward Launcelot Davey Cole, appointed as an assistant master in 1898; retired from the school in 1935.

51 Lord Porchester had previously been a pupil at Eton before joining Rugby in 1913. Dr Edward Lyttelton was headmaster of Eton from 1905–16. His tenure was highly controversial, culminating in a furore over a sermon he delivered in 1915 suggesting there should be a negotiated peace. He resigned in 1916 amid publicity given to the prosecution of his German maid on a dubious charge of spying.

52 Frank Alexander de Pass (Brooke's 1901–4); served with 34th Poona Horse, Indian Army; awarded the VC for conspicuous bravery near Festubert on 24 November 1914, in entering a German sap and destroying a traverse in the face of the enemy's bombs, and for subsequently rescuing, under heavy fire, a wounded man who was lying exposed in the open. In a second attempt to capture the German sap, which had been re-occupied by the enemy, de Pass was killed. He was also mentioned in despatches twice.

53 Martin Bateson (SH 1913–17): served with RFC and died on 22 April, 1922.

54 Lieutenant-Colonel Sir Edward Henry Clarke.

55 Graham de Montmorency Armstrong-Lushington-Tulloch (Donkin's 1900–3): served with 1st Bn Connaught Rangers; killed at Neuve Chapelle on 5 November, 1914.

56 For a detailed analysis of the cause of riots in 1915, see P. Panayi, 'Anti-German riots in Britain during the First World War', in P. Panayi (Ed), *Racial Violence in Britain, 1840–1950* (Leicester, 1993).

57 James Trevor Crawley Vincent (Stallard's 1909–13): served with 3rd Bn Welsh Regt; killed near Ypres on 9 May, 1915.

58 James Cartmell Dennison Brown (SH 1907–12): served with 5th Bn Durham Light Infantry; died of wounds received at the second Battle of Ypres, 27 April, 1915.

59 Norris Carden Bretherton (SH 1913–16): died in an aeroplane accident in India in June, 1925.

60 Conrad Powell Johnstone (Steel's 1910–13): served with 1st Bn Highland Light Infantry; wounded twice, but went on to win Cricket Blues at Cambridge University in 1919 and 1920.

61 John Russell Benham (Whitelaw's 1909–13): served with 100th Battery RGA; died of wounds received at Ypres, 4 May, 1915.

62 John Solomon Riddell Hodgson (SH 1910–14): served with 2nd Bn Dorsetshire Regt; wounded in 1915, and later killed in Mesopotamia on 25 March, 1917.

63 Ian Nevill Fyfe-Jamieson (Whitelaw's 1909–12): served with the 2nd Bn Seaforth Highlanders; awarded the Croix de Guerre and mentioned in despatches twice.

64 Alan Francis Vertue (G.F. Bradby's 1908–13): served with 1st Bn HAC; died of wounds received at St Eloi, on 21 April, 1915.

65 Stanley Attenborough (SH 1912–15): served with 22nd Brigade RFA.

66 John Lindsay Bryan (Stallard's 1911–14): served with 1st Bn HAC, 5th Bn Manchester Regt and 42nd Bn Machine Gun Corps; awarded MC.

67 Agricultural work became a regular feature of life in Rugby School in the War. During the term pupils helped local farmers, and in the holidays formed agricultural camps in various parts of the country. See Collis, *Silver Fleece*, pp.59–65.

68 A.H. Pollen, who lectured on 'The British Navy at War'.

69 Samuel Holt Lomax (Hutchinson's 1869–74): served with 1st and 2nd Bns Cameronians (Scottish Rifles), and GHQ Staff; awarded CB and mentioned in despatches; died on 10 April, 1915, following wounds sustained in France, when a shell fell in the midst of a group of Staff Officers attending a conference in the Château of La Hooge. Five officers were killed, including Lieutenant-General Lomax and Lieutenant-Colonel A. Percival, OR, (see Note 44. above).

70 The Field Day was held at Fenny Compton with The Oratory and King Edward's, Birmingham.

71 Thomas William Jex-Blake was a pupil at Rugby School from 1844–8, before returning as an assistant master 1858–68. He was Principal of Cheltenham College from 1868–74, and headmaster of Rugby 1874–87.

72 Henry Morrant Stanford (SH 1908–12): served with 32nd Battery RFA; awarded the MC, Croix de Guerre and mentioned in despatches.

73 Christopher Llewellyn Bullock (Town 1904–10): served with 6th Bn Rifle Brigade, and later RFC; awarded OBE and mentioned in despatches.

74 Edward Charles Iles (SH 1913–17): served with RFC.

75 Frederick James Kittermaster was appointed as an assistant master in 1902, served as a housemaster 1914–29 and retired in 1934.

76 See Note 31. above.

77 John Stephen Cawley (SH 1894–7): served with 1st Cavalry Division,

20th Hussars; mentioned in despatches; killed in Nery in the retreat from Mons, 1 September, 1914

78 C.A. Alington, headmaster of Shrewsbury, and later Eton. The poem is quoted in Parker, *The Old Lie*, p.257.

79 John Owen Iles (SH 1907–12): served with 1st Bn South Staffordshire Regt, attached to 1st Bn Royal Welsh Fusiliers; killed at Loos, 25 September, 1915.

80 Rev H. Ward.

81 John Alfred Pigon Inglis (Collins' 1907–11): served with Royal Engineers; killed at Loos 25 September, 1915.

82 Douglas Kirk Wolley-Dod (SH 1910–14): served with 12th Bn Liverpool Regt; killed near Laventie, 25 September, 1915.

PART THREE

LOUIS STOKES AT WAR

January–November 1916

Louis sat the scholarship examination for Corpus Christi, Cambridge, in December, 1915. His mind was already firmly set on joining the War, and it was therefore no surprise that he was unsuccessful in the examination. The greatest disappointment would have been felt by Louis' father, who had always hoped that his son would achieve success as a scholar, a disappointment compounded by fears for his only son's safety and his own anti-militarist views.

It had been in early December, 1915, that Louis had told Dr David that he wished to join the Royal Marines, expressing a desire to go to sea. The necessary papers had been requested from the Admiralty, and by 6th January, 1916, Louis, aged eightteen, was in uniform and beginning his training at Forton Barracks, Gosport. He would have had little difficulty being accepted into the Royal Marines: there was a manpower shortage, he had been to a famous public school and he had been a member of an O.T.C. for fifteen months. Others did not find things quite so easy. R.C. Sherriff, author of *Journey's End*, described his first attempt to become an officer in August, 1914:

'School?' enquired the adjutant. I told him and his face fell. He took up a printed list and searched through it. 'I'm sorry,' he said, 'but I'm afraid it isn't a public school.' I was mystified. I told him that my school, though small, was a very old and good one – founded, I said, by Queen Elizabeth in 1567. The adjutant was not impressed. He had lost all interest in me.[1]

Despite such arbitrary rejections, there was a grave shortage of suitably trained officers to cope with the vast numbers of volunteer recruits who flooded into the services in 1914–15. In September, 1914, nearly half a million men volunteered for the Army, all of whom needed suitable officers to command them.[2] As a consequence, retired Indian cavalrymen, militia colonels and disabled pensioners were often called into service.[3] An instruction from the Secretary of State for War on 6 September, 1914, told those in charge of local recruitment to demand from Post Offices the names and addresses of everyone who received a letter addressed to 'Colonel', 'Major', 'Captain', or 'Lieutenant', to see if they had already sent in their names. If not, a 'civil letter' was to be written inviting the retired officer to do so, 'in such a manner that he can hardly refuse'.[4]

The Royal Marines, which Louis had chosen to join, had originally been raised in 1664 with the role of reinforcing the personnel of the Royal Navy, which involved such duties as providing landing parties, manning secondary armaments, and providing small arms fire. At the outbreak of War the Royal Marines had 407 serving officers and a total complement of 18,234 men.[5] These totals hid 'a most serious shortage of trained officers', and the Royal Marines Light Infantry had a shortfall of thirty-nine officers. On 2 August, 1914, the Reserves were called out and the mobilization went smoothly. The King's Pardon was granted to all deserters who reported for service, and 'a very considerable number surrendered themselves'.[6] One Royal Marine, who had deserted in the East Indies, had then gone to inland Mexico to work. He only heard of the War in February, 1915, and worked his passage to Liverpool where he arrived penniless. He then walked to Deal and joined his Division.[7]

By March, 1915, the Royal Marines had grown to 33,116 men with 705 officers; by the end of the War the total complement was 55,603 with 1,271 officers.[8] Recruiting had proved relatively easy in the early months of the War, as with all branches of the armed forces, and the Royal Marines soon made good their shortfall with the help of calling up many over-aged reservists, and also giving commissions to many NCOs and warrant officers already serving. The temporary officers (such as Louis) were largely drawn from the universities and public schools, the Inns of Court OTC and, after the transfer of the Royal Naval Division to France, officers from the Officer Cadet Battalions of the Army who volunteered for service with the Royal Marines.[9] By the end of 1915, when Louis joined the Royal Marines, the flow of voluntary recruits had been fast drying up; there is no doubt that he would have been welcomed with open arms.

After his training at Portsmouth and Blandford, Louis was to join the 2nd Battalion of the Royal Marines Light Infantry, which had been posted to France in May, 1916, as part of the Royal Naval Division, after seeing action in the Gallipoli campaign. A fierce controversy had been raging in Britain over the control of the Royal Naval Division. The Admiralty wanted to be rid of its responsibility for the Division, whilst the War Office wanted to mould it on the lines of one of the New Army Divisions, thus destroying its distinctive Naval characteristics. Sir Edward Carson, First Lord of the Admiralty, prevented this, although the War Office assumed responsibility for recruitment, maintenance, training and discipline. The Admiralty retained the appointment of officers to commissions, and control over pay and allowances.[10].

The Royal Naval Division was a strange hybrid, intensely proud of its naval traditions, yet forced to wear khaki and tin hats. The Division, renamed the 63rd (Royal Naval) Division in July, 1916, considered itself to be 'something special, a cut above mere soldiers with their kow-towing khaki discipline'.[11] Their Divisional Commander was General A. Paris, who had gone on record as saying, 'Man for man and officer for officer the Naval Division is incomparably better than nine-tenths of the Divisions in France'.[12] In October, 1916, General Paris was severely wounded and succeeded by General C. Shute, whose lack of confidence in the Division was matched only by the men's lack of respect for their new Commanding Officer.[13]

After leaving the Mediterranean on 7 May, 1916, and docking at Marseilles on 12 May, 2/RMLI were first posted to Longpré, where they remained until the end of May, 1916, training and being re-equipped. The Battalion then transferred to Hersin and underwent training in trench routine with the 47th Division. They were operating in the Angres-Souchez sector of the line, and subsequently on the Bajolles-Maistre line of defence. On 29 June 2/RMLI relieved 1/RMLI in the front line trenches of the Angres II subsector. This section of the line lay in front of the heights of Notre Dame de Lorette which had been captured by the French in 1915. By this period of the war the systems of holding the front line and support lines in strength had been abandoned. Artillery fire was now the key to defence, whilst the front and support lines became in effect a line of sentry groups and a line of pickets. There was still lateral communication by means of a continuous trench, but a line of posts became the normal first line. The support line was the first line for delaying action and holding up local attack. The third line was generally the main line of resistance, which was held by two companies on a battalion front of 600–800 yards, with dug-out protection, machine-gun and trench mortar emplacements.

Louis continued his training and departed for France on 7 July, 1916. He joined his battalion on 11 July and was in the front-line trenches within a week. From 14 July, 1916, to 20 September, 1916, the two RMLI battalions relieved each other in the front line of the Angres II subsector. The usual routine was to spend four days in the front line, moving then to the reserve for three days, a day in the support line, and then back to the front line.

Conditions in the trenches were appalling, although Louis made light of this when writing home. He mentioned the vast number of rats, and this is confirmed by the Corps history: 'The trenches were swarming with rats and great rat hunts were instituted.'[14] In addition, the trenches were muddy and wet, even in August, yet fresh water for drinking was always in short supply. It had to be carried to the front line from the support lines by parties of two or three men using petrol tins, 'although sometimes too much petrol had been left in'.[15] The trenches cannot have been particularly well-maintained, because, although Louis commented on the beauty of overhanging archways of flowers, this was a sign of neglected maintenance.[16]

On 20 September, 1916, 2/RMLI left the line for further training (Louis was on a signalling course at this time), moving first to Beguin and then to Mouchy Bretton. On 4 October the battalion travelled to Acheux and went into billets in Englebelmer, where Louis rejoined them, in preparation to take part in the Battle of the Somme, which had been raging since 1 July.

The failure of the initial attack and the catastrophic felling of Kitchener's volunteer forces have been well documented elsewhere.[17] It has been persuasively argued that, if the German Army could have chosen anywhere to receive an attack it would probably have been on the Somme. By the summer of 1916 'every hilltop was a redoubt, every wood was an arsenal, every farm a stronghold, every village a fortress'.[18] On 1 July, 57,000 British soldiers had become casualties; 20,000 of them dead.

With the benefit of hindsight, the question to be asked now would be whether the attack should have continued after 1 July. For the British command the question was rather where the attack should continue. On 14 July the British launched their second substantial attack of the Somme campaign, when a force of 20,000 men captured Longueval Ridge. In the following days there was less to celebrate, as the new tactic of limited sector attacks concentrated all the enemy's reserves. Gradually, however, during the weeks that followed, Pozières, Guillemont, Delville Wood and Thiepval all fell in what had now become a war of attrition. R. H. Tawney[19], Old Rugbeian, described his feelings in the Somme campaign as being 'like a merry mischievous ape tearing up the image of God'.[20] Between July and September, 1916, 90,000 men were killed on the Somme and 228,632 were sent wounded to base camps.[21]

By the end of September, 1916, except for a small section north of Thiepval, the whole of that crest of ground which had been at the core of the Allies' objectives on 1 July was in British hands. There seemed few logical reasons for continuing the campaign after this date, especially as the weather broke on 2 October and it rained for most of the month. Louis, like most soldiers at the front, made light of the appalling conditions in which they were forced to exist. Haig decided to continue the campaign on the basis that German morale was near to breaking point and that a significant breakthrough was still possible. His initial optimism was rewarded when Thiepval Ridge and Le Sars had both been captured by the end of October.

The attack at Beaumont Hamel on 13 November, in which Louis was to lose his life, was an even greater act of optimism by Haig, and indeed was little more than a gamble. The German Army had undoubtedly settled down for the winter, and a surprise attack, when it was least expected, might easily accomplish a significant victory. The weather had also improved, and the thunderstorms and torrential rain of October had given way to bright and sunny autumnal days. However, the reasons for the late offensive were rather more diplomatic than military. On 15 November Haig was due to meet with the French High Command at Chantilly to decide the future strategy of the War. The French were pressing the British to continue their attacks to prevent the Germans switching any manpower to reinforce positions at Verdun. A victory at Beaumont Hamel would strengthen the British hand at the Chantilly Conference.

2/RMLI had been awaiting their first offensive action on the western front since their arrival in France six months earlier. They were living in bivouacs in a 'strip of sheer desolation'[22], sodden by rain, and without even coats for protection.[23] Many availed themselves of the old Marine privilege and grew beards, and an issue of cardigans on 7 November was very welcome. To the disgust of the RMLI 'someone in authority had a brain wave; and issued pea flour every alternate night instead of the rum.'[24]

On 12 November at 2.00 pm 2/RMLI moved to their battle stations, ready to take part in what has become known as the Battle of the Ancre. As part of the 63rd Division, V Corps, their objective was Beaucourt and the intervening positions, on the north bank of the River Ancre. During the night 2/RMLI moved into positions in the open and at 5.45 am on 13 November began their attack in pitch dark and thick mist. They were in the second line and it was intended that they would leap-frog the first line and eventually take Beaucourt and establish a defensive flank on the left of the attack.[25] A barrage preceded the initial attack and, despite considerable German machine-gun fire and the glutinous mud, the front system was captured. 2/RMLI moved forward and apparently crossed the line dribbling a football, despite 'one continual mass of débris and mud, and pools, some half-filled with water and many badly wounded men lying helpless'.[26] They were involved in hand-to-hand fighting, but by 11.00 am had reached what was known as the Green Line, beyond the road which ran between Beaucourt Station and Beaumont Hamel. By 11.00 am also, Louis Stokes, aged nineteen, was dead.

In the three days which followed, St Pierre Divion, Beaucourt and Beaumont Hamel were all captured, and in that sense Haig's gamble had paid off. After the first snowstorms of the winter, the Somme campaign was brought to an end on 19 November, 1916. The British had lost 420,000 men, yet nowhere did they advance more than ten miles from their start line on 1 July. Despite a military effort unparalleled in the history of British warfare, the

Somme campaign had failed to inflict a strategic defeat on the enemy.

In the last letter Louis had sent home, he wrote: 'I wish I could tell you what we are doing, but I can't. However, I am having great fun, as I hope you are.'[27] The final entry in the diary of a brother officer in 2/RMLI, who also lost his life on 13 November, was perhaps more apt: 'We are waiting . . . pray for us all at this time. We need your prayers. God help us.'[28]

Forton Barracks
Gosport
Hants
[Postmarked: 6 January 1916]

Dear all,

As I have told you, I got here all right. When I got out at Portsmouth Harbour I was saluted by a huge Marine who inquired if I was coming to the Forton barracks, and then showed me the way up. Portsmouth harbour is amazing to me, big ships lying about and Nelson's 'Victory,' a few hundred yards out from the quay, seagulls flying about. Hundreds of sailors, marines and soldiers who salute you from many yards away. You get into a steamboat which takes you across the harbour past big buoys . . . I went down into Gosport and got my hat badge put right, feeling very small when great sergeants saluted me and sentries came smartly to the 'shun', and passed various barracks. Then I came back and went into the officers' mess and sat down and read papers. There were only three officers there as nearly everyone else was on leave. One officer (a lieutenant risen from the ranks) had the decency to say good afternoon. I felt a bit out of place, but after a bit another temporary arrived called Clanchy, a very decent chap. After some tea we reported ourselves to the adjutant whom we found in his shirtsleeves pasting pictures, picture-postcards, etc on a screen for his small daughter. He was very decent to us and we helped him do his screen . . . This adj told us that we should stay here probably for three to four months, after which we might be drafted to the front, possibly Servia, but since the Dardanelles business had stopped we might stay here longer. Tomorrow we start work, he told us, which will be drill at 8.15 for an hour. A bit later physical drill for which we shall need *white flannel trousers* which you might send at the earliest opportunity and send the bill to me. Then a lecture till lunch and 2–4 in the afternoon something else.

After mess dinner (7.45) at which there were only two or three officers, I and Clanchy went down to Portsmouth and to the shore and saw the Isle of Wight in the distance and all sorts of red and white lights between Hayling Island and the Isle of Wight where there is a great harbour barrier. Then we went back to barracks and to bed (11 o'clock).

This morning, breakfast (8), Church parade, to which the temporaries marched off independently after falling in. Here we met some more temporaries, eight or ten, very decent men. Rotten service and hopeless chaplain, whose name I don't know or want to. Mechanical service, praying, singing etc. No one in the least interested. Then went on another walk with Clanchy to Portsmouth and had lunch. Clanchy is awfully decent; he has been in the Merchant Marine and can tell one all about ships which he does very willingly. He was wrecked off Cornwall and just after that a new order for sight-testing came out (like those changing coloured lights I had at the Admiralty) and he was turned out because he could not pass it.

Now I will close. Thank you for all your various services before I went, too numerous to mention in detail.

I will tell you more when I know more.

Yrs with love,
Louis.

R.M.L.I
Forton Barracks
Gosport
[Postmarked: 19 January 1916]

Dear Mother,

Please excuse pencil, as I am writing this in my 'quarters' (private room, that is), and have not bought any ink yet.

. . . I am going to be inoculated on Friday afternoon, and the adjutant advised us to put in for leave during the weekend . . . So I thought I would come home, although I have only just left, because then I can get anything I have not already got that I want

. . . Also, as I have now pretty well settled down, I shall like to review the situation in the quietness of my native abode. After which I shall return I hope, to a good long go at it during which I shall not see you.

. . . On Sunday night I went to Portsmouth parish church (St Mary's) with Clanchy . . . as I knew Dr David's brother[29] (who preached to us in the summer term at Rugby) is vicar there.

. . . On Monday, we paraded at 8.15 (breakfast 7.30) with the other eight temporaries who have been here about a fortnight. And while they did very elementary drill Clanchy and I were taken off to be shown how to fit a soldier's equipment on (which we have to wear for drill purposes) . . . Then gym, which we were told to watch, as we had not got trousers to wear . . . Then a long lecture till just before dinner by a Colonel Evans, who is a funny old chap but knows what he is talking about . . . After dinner we paraded at 2.00 and were instructed in elementary drill, which I really did know ridiculously well . . . from 3–4 we had signalling practice, morse code with flags (and more of this with lamps from 6–7).

love Louis.

Forton Barracks
Gosport
Hants
[Postmarked: 31 January 1916]

Dear all,

. . . My routine is not very exciting, being drill 8.15 to 10.30 with a $\frac{1}{4}$ hr's break, and 11–12.30, lecture on field work. Then in the afternoon 2–3 and 3–4 either drill or lecture or drill and signalling or drill and drill. This is the routine regularly for every day. The exceptions are that on Wednesdays there is a route march parading at 8 a.m. and finishing at about 2.30 at the earliest, and on Fridays a 3/6d expedition into the country for fieldwork parading at 9.30 at the station and home about 3.00.

On Saturdays there is nothing after 12.30 and Church Parade on Sunday at 9.00. Every evening there is mess dinner for all who are not billeted out; this you must attend unless you ask the Mess President for leave off . . .

Breakfast in the morning at 7.30. I get my servant to call me at 6.30. I have a new servant now as Crooke had too many men to manage . . . Crooke's wife does my washing. I have had my first lot from her, a shirt, two handkerchiefs, two towels, pyjamas, socks for 1/-. I don't know if that is a moderate price. It seems to me to be so. They are done all right. On Wednesday the Adjutant General of the Marines Sir John Nicholls is coming down to inspect us (if that interests you) . . .

With love to all,
Louis.

Forton barracks
Gosport
[Postmarked: 15 February 1916]

Dear all,
    . . . Will you please send a *little dark red* book of mine called 'Musketry Regulations 1914', which I think you will find on the chest of drawers in the dressing room . . . I had it at Rugby for the O.T.C. and need it here. It is all about shooting with a rifle or machine gun and is a very important part of training as of course victory depends a great deal upon who can incapacitate the most men, which is horrible . . . I drew my first pay a fortnight ago tomorrow, £16.13.0 made up, according to receipt, of £13.10.0 Pay, £3.3.0 War Allowance (whatever that may be). My mess bill for the fortnight of January was £3.8.9 . . . This week I am Mess President and feel a perfect ass sitting at the head of the table with Majors and people floating around. However, I must put up with it. Fortunately on my right hand today sat a temporary Lieutenant who has been to Gallipoli who was in School House Rugby, I discovered, at least he discovered it to me. His name is Belton,[30] I think, but I am not sure. He has only come in today. He is taking a course of gunnery here preparatory I suppose to going on a ship. This was most interesting as he knew well a fellow at Rugby I liked very much who was wounded in Flanders. A bullet went in his ear, down his mouth and into his lung. He breathes out of one lung now. He knew a good deal about Rugby though he was only there 1 term, then he went to St Paul's and Cambridge I think. A decent man, a good deal older than I am, as he was at Rugby in 1897.
    . . . I have heard some funny stories. There is a Colonel here called Col. Matthews, who has a great string of ribbons across his chest and is a great friend of Kitchener, who thinks a lot of him.

He went with the Portsmouth Battalion to the Dardanelles. I have heard two accounts of his behaviour there which are interesting as coming from two very different points of view. The first was from our drill instructor, a quartermaster sergt, a splendid man (he was a sergt major in Gallipoli but they always take away those temporary ranks when they come back – he had a platoon there). This man went to Anzac, the worst place of the lot in Gallipoli and saw some awful things. He was wounded. He said, 'a man told me that Colonel Matthews walked about on the beach at Anzac just as if he was on parade with shells and bullets flying all round him, taking no notice'.

The other account was from Colonel Evans . . . He has been up in the Shetland Islands organizing the defences up there till about two months ago, but he has never been in action anywhere . . . He said, 'I believe Colonel Matthews ought to be a dead man several times over through exposing himself unnecessarily. Several people have told me that.'

Yours with love,
Louis.

P.S.   I enclose £19.2.6. for bills and 5d in stamps for the postage of book.

Forton Barracks
Gosport, Hants
[Postmarked: 28 February 1916]

Dear all,
      . . . I went across to Portsmouth to church. Like you and everyone else we have had a lot of snow. Today it was thawing slightly, tho' still cold. However, all the way to Portsmouth it snowed hard, though a wet sleety kind of snow, and it was a wet crossing of the Harbour. There is a great big battleship lying in the Dockyard now. I always enjoy this crossing very much; it is worth more than 1/2d to me. The gulls alone are wonderful, with their black heads and grey wings, wheeling and falling on the water, and screaming as they do. I always think of all the ships you see in the Harbour, and I have seen most kinds from the *Mauretania* which

lay alongside the *Aquitania* in the Solent last week, to a Lowestoft trawler. The *Victory* is far the finest, with her broad spread of yardarms and great sides . . .

love Louis.

Forton Barracks
Gosport, Hants
[Postmarked: 16 March 1916]

Dear all,

 . . . Routine goes on much as usual, of course getting a little more advanced by the day. It is interesting work, and I begin to feel more of an officer than I did at first. But it will be fine when the war ends, though I should think it will be a good while after that before the army will be demobilized. The officers here are all decent, some very decent indeed, and our instructors are all splendid men.

 . . . I had another splendid letter from Mr Raven. They all have German measles at Rugby. Phillips,[31] a Lieutenant here who lives in Rugby and was there with me, went home on leave for the week-end. He reports that, by way of economy, *all tuckshops* are out of bounds after nine o'clock in the morning! A severe blow for some boys! Not to mention the unfortunate tuckshop keepers who live on the School's demand practically.

 Another economy is that there is to be no more caps, badges or any other pompous paraphernalia. *Another economy* – this a really surprising one, is that each holiday is to be increased by one week. Thus nine weeks in the summer, five weeks at Christmas and Easter!!! This is because the Housemasters must make their profit on house fees, but as food prices are going up so high, they are going to keep the fees the same, and have more holidays. Just when I've left of course!

 I am very glad indeed to hear that you have got a curate at last . . .

Now I will shut off,
love to all,
Louis.

Forton Barracks
Gosport
[Postmarked: 20 March 1916]

Dear all,

. . . It is interesting to meet various men here who have been in fights or disasters at sea . . . The other day I was talking to a sergeant who was in a ship within 100 yards of the *Natal* when she blew up, or down rather, for he said she was sucked under not blown up by the explosion. His ship got the first boats on the scene. He worked the davits – you know those things they let the boats down by. You remember the *Natal* was the ship there was a children's party on at the time. He said he didn't think any women or children were saved, he didn't see any. The captain's quarters, where they were, are nearly always *aft* in a ship, and the explosion took place aft. He said it was dreadful to see people swimming about, and just as they got near a boat, stop swimming thinking they would catch hold of the boat's side, and go straight under exhausted. He said he saw lots do that . . .

Now I will say goodbye. Hoping you will have a good week.

Love to all. Thank you for your letters,
Louis.

Forton Barracks
Gosport, Hants
[Undated: mid-May 1916]

Dear all,

. . . I, with my platoon, have been digging trenches, marching, and shooting this week; also some bombing. When I am digging I sometimes think of Newport five weeks back, and of how we all watched the Scotchman dig – how I wish to be there . . . I should like you to see the Marines at work. Better than those Scotch fellows . . . I saw two little girls in black in Portsmouth this evening; I am afraid their father must be 'somewhere in the North Sea' . . .

Now goodbye,
with love from Louis.

Forton Barracks
Gosport, Hants
[Postmarked: 23 May 1916]

Dear all,

. . . On Friday last nine of us (temporary officers) were asked in official letters whether we would elect to be trained in the corps afloat instead of for service with the Royal Naval Division. We all said 'no' at once, but next day the adjutant gave me a private jaw in which he stated that he strongly advised me to accept. He seemed to think it was a great chance, chiefly, I think, because he thought I had no particular profession in mind and this was a good opportunity. He was very decent about it, and it was kind of him to trouble at all about it. I told him I should like to think over it, which I did and decided to stick by my original decision, and go for service ashore with the R.N.D. When I joined the Marines of course I wanted to go to sea, but I have since changed my mind. If I went to sea, I should not get on a ship till the beginning of next year, whilst the Naval Division may be in France in a few months. I think it would be rather lazy to go to sea as matters stand. I don't know what you think . . .

love to all,
Louis.

Forton Barracks
Gosport, Hants
[Postmarked: 1 June 1916]

Dear all,

. . . I have been given a platoon and they are going through musketry. I am in charge of them . . . though of course I do not instruct them in musketry, as there are special men for that purpose (and I don't know much about it).

I am going through musketry again, as I am up there. My platoon's living there under canvas, but I go up on a bike every morning from barracks and come back in the afternoon, as I prefer having a bit of each kind of surroundings.

My platoon goes by the name of the 31st platoon. They are a splendid lot of men, but there are only twenty-five of them and a corporal. And I think it very likely that when we have finished

147

training we shall be sent to fill up other platoons and not form a separate one. Of course I shall try to keep my men. They are all shooting very well, better than I do, most of them.

. . . I was out with Browning,[32] yesterday afternoon and went to a theatre with him in the evening. 'The Glad Eye'; it was very funny, but I do not care for theatre, except as a sort of medicine once a month.

Browning is a splendid chap, none better. He has a motorbike and takes me on the back. We go along pitching frightfully. Great fun.

Now good luck to all,
and love from
Louis.

Forton Barracks
Gosport, Hants
[Postmarked: 8 June 1916]

Dear all,

. . . There are many sad homes in Portsmouth and Gosport this week, as the three big ships were Portsmouth vessels. On Tuesday three survivors came in off the destroyer *Tipperary*. They were dressed in any old clothes, with sailors' caps on with *HMS Sparrowhawk* on the ribbon. They were sunk on *HMS Tipperary* and picked up by the *Sparrowhawk* which was sunk in its turn. They say the *Tipperary* was hit in the bows by one of our own vessles by mistake, and finally rammed as she was sinking by another vessel, again by mistake!

We are to move within a week or two now I think; a good job . . .

Love to all,
Louis.

Forton Barracks
Gosport, Hants
[Postmarked: 20 June 1916]

Dear all,

. . . On the 28th June, we are to go to a place called Blandford in Dorsetshire, to join the Royal Naval Division. We are to form a

Reserve Battalion to the Royal Marine Battalion now serving as part of the R.N.D. with the French at or near Verdun. From Blandford we shall be drafted to the front as they require us.

This will be a change of air and scenery, but not routine. But I like Portsmouth very much, especially the Harbour, and shall be sorry to leave it. My routine now is digging, marching, trenchfighting (bombing particularly).

I saw a very fine ship come into Harbour last week; it was the battle-cruiser *Princess Royal*, (of HMS *Queen Mary* class), which was sunk in the Jutland battle, so the Germans said. I was fortunate to see her; she is one of the biggest ships of war afloat, though only a battle-*cruiser*, that is built for speed as well as gunpower, and not a battle-*ship* like HMS *Queen Elizabeth*, which is built for gunpower chiefly . . . You would never imagine that there would be such a big ship; it looked as though it would not be able to get into St Paul's Road, unless Fenner's wall was removed and our garden, and the churchyard and the alms houses and so on done likewise to. All the crew, (what was left of them), were lined up on board and they cheered time and again as they passed the *Victory* and again as they turned into the dock. I hear she was a good deal damaged (in the bows, after funnel, after turret and port quarter) but I did not notice this. It is the only ship I have seen coming in from the battle. I have seen many families in black here in Portsmouth.

At the air station near here they have just discovered three spies, an officer and two men, who had been occupying their time in loosening nuts and screws on the aeroplanes, with the result that they have had about ten killed this year . . .

Now I will say goodbye,
Hoping to see you on Saturday or Friday,
love to all,
Louis.

Royal Marines
Royal Naval Camp
Blandford
[Postmarked: 2 July 1916]

Dear all,
    . . . Well we arrived at Blandford after a good send-off at

Gosport by the population, and here we are. We are 3 ½ miles from Blandford up on the downs in the direction of Salisbury. Where we are is an absolutely ripping place. I do not remember anywhere like it except perhaps the hills behind the vicarage at Childerditch or the downs at Hunstanton where we once went in a donkey cart. From west to east there is about ¾ mile on each side of us of open down, rolling up and down with nothing in the way of it. On the eastern horizon, certain clumps of trees and a lot of black huts, where the Naval Divison are. On the western horizon are more trees and more huts; these last huts are the hospital. In the middle we are; about a hundred tents, besides about fifty R.N.D. tents. North of us, the downs go up to the skyline, and about a mile away . . . they roll down into a cultivated land of hill and lake looking very pretty, though the corn is still green. There are miles of huge corn-fields and turnip fields and ploughed fields, and here a wood and there a little village among trees. It is absolutely topping and nothing shuts out the sky all round. The air is searching usually, hot sometimes when the sun has been shining for long . . . and really cold at night. Already I have been for three long walks among the fields by myself. I very much enjoy it, sleep beautifully, and though I do not wake up any earlier, am not sleepy when I wake. Our routine is parade at 6.15, physical training for all till 7 o'clock, breakfast 7.30, then from 8.45 till 4.30 in the afternoon – with 1½ break for dinner (12.30–1) – we do all sorts of field training, (that's training for service in the field and includes everything that you want to know about active service except the real thing) . . .

Now goodbye,
with love from Louis.

[Telegram: sent at 0635, 5 July 1916]

Going to France Friday coming home today please have some breakfast for me between 9.30 and 10

Stokes

Infantry Base Depot
Royal Naval Division
A[rmy].P[ost].O[office].S.17
B.E.F.
8 July 1916

Dear all,

I am at this moment in my tent on some hills at a place in cis-alpine Gaul of which, for military reasons, it is inexpedient to say anything further; (ahem), beyond that we heard the guns roaring in the distance this morning, so I suppose we are less than 100 miles from the battle line.

My train got to London in fairly good time but the train at Charing Cross was packed, and several of us had to go down in a 3rd class carriage, with some Derby recruits.[33]

We had a smooth crossing. We passed three lightships, with no names on that I could see. One of them, near France, was painted up all red and white stripes like a circus girl.

When we landed at – we had about six hours to wait before our train started. Reporting ourselves and seeing to our gear took a long time. Then we (I and Dewar) had supper in a place for British Officers. The French servants and ways were very amusing; the food was good. Then we took a walk round, through dark cobbled streets with old high houses on either side looking strange and romantic in the clear evening dusk; past little leaping and scream-ing French girls and boys and dark handsome mothers and French policemen and soldiers in their unfamiliar uniform. After a bit we passed under a dark gloomy archway and turned into a sort of avenue or grove of mighty trees with grass leading up to a stone, ancient-looking building on one side, and to a great stone wall on the other, in places wide enough to drive a horse and cart along, with semi-circular embrasures which we leant over and saw through the branches of high dark trees, a road 100ft below glowing white. It was now quite dusk, and this strange old grove seemed to us very romantic and typical of old France that you read of. And as we lay in the grass watching a blood-orange sunset over the fortified wall, a lovely light shone on a river far in the distance. Then, like Little Shenford bells, from the ancient stone building the bells rang for mass. . . . I slept well in the train, and we arrived here at about 4.30. I slept till 8.30 about, then went into the village or

151

town and had omelettes, bread and cafe au lait at the hotel. Today, we have slept mostly, feeding from time to time. This afternoon we have got into tents and got our gear straight . . .

I do not know how long we are to stay here or anything about it. Please note address. Copy it exactly without additions.

love to you all,
from Louis.

2nd Battalion
Royal Marine Brigade
B.E.F. France
12th July, [1916] Wednesday

Dear all,

Last night we had orders to join the R.M. Brigade up in front.

We therefore drew certain rations, known as iron rations. consisting of bully beef, dog biscuits, etc., packed up and after a rather hurried breakfast at 3 a.m. this morning left – by a train supposed to start at 4.30 a.m., actually 5.00.

We travelled until about 12.15 making stops of about half an hour every three quarters of an hour or so. What happened when we stopped no one quite knows. The engine seemed to be removed and we went backwards and forwards several times, but I suppose there was a useful purpose behind it. We were all very sleepy, and only woke from time to time to watch the country we were passing through. France seems to my eyes a more delicate kind of scenery than England, fields and trees and houses seem more soft and graceful . . . There are funny little carriages on the trains. At the close of our train journey we approached a town from which crowds of little school children emerged and raced along the side of the train – which during the whole journey did not often go much more than 20 m.p.h., and at this point went at about 7 m.p.h. – shouting, 'souvenir, souvenir'. They received a good many presents of various descriptions, from ten centime pieces to tins of bully beef.

From this town we were taken to our present position in great motor lorries, very powerful as they carried all our gear and a lot of us, and went at a great pace. We got coated with white dust. I have never seen so much dust as there is here.

This place is a few miles behind the firing line in the neighbourhood of _____[34], (if you know where that is). It is within range of German gunfire, but very unlikely to be hit as it is protected to a large extent by a great hill which goes up immediately above our position.[35] This makes it very difficult for the Germans to put a shell into us as their guns are a fair distance off, and of course shells begin to drop after about half way through the air. We can hear our own guns and German ones strafing away.

Coming up we passed a house destroyed by shell fire. We saw too one of those crucifixes by the roadside in a hedge that you read of. It is grand fun here and we are going up into the firing line tomorrow to take our turn there for four or five days. At least we are marching up tomorrow, and relieving the troops at present there on Friday. Of course I am looking forward to this . . .

I saw one of the London buses used for transport out here that we have heard so much of . . . We did *gassing* [for two days before moving into the line], practising with helmets on, and going through a gas trench with them on, and bayonet fighting. You would be surprised at how difficult it is to breath with the gas helmets on, especially if you exert yourself.

Hope you are all well. I will now close. Wishing good luck to all of you and to myself. I hope to be able to report myself safe and sound next week.

> love to you all,
> Louis.

> 2nd Battalion
> Royal Marines
> B.E.F. France
> 26th July 1916

Dear all,

My last letter to you was written on the day before I went up to the trenches. This one is written on the day after I came down. Knock off a day at each end for going up and down, and you will see how long I was there [11 days]. Divide this by two and you will know how long I was in the reserve line and how long in the firing line.

. . . The day after I wrote to you we started off all loaded up like Santa Claus and with our steel shrapnel helmets on. We went about five miles and then put up for the night at a village. It had a few ruins in it, but was not shelled at all then. The men were billeted in an empty convent, and I with Dewar and another chap, over an estaminet, which is the same thing as a public house in England. Very interesting it was.

Next day we marched another five miles and after a bit turned off the road into a cornfield, up a trench. After going along this trench for a long way we came to the line we had to hold. We then stowed the men away in dugouts and looked at ours. It was a very elaborate one; it is sometimes used as a Brigade H[ead] Quarters and we were using it as a Company H.Q., only five of us. There were steps leading into it; what I mean is that the ordinary dugout for men goes straight down into the earth, but ours had steps leading down to the door of the dugout, *then* you go below the earth. On the right hand side of the steps was a raised sort of terrace with a seat. In the dugout was a sort of room to the right with two beds with wire springs on each side, a room with one bed to the left, and a parlour in the middle with a mantelpiece and mirror over it. In the wall by the fireplace a deep dugout went down twenty ft, and there another bed at the bottom of this. There we spent quite a happy time, eating and sleeping by day, and working at improving trenches further towards the firing line (which was about 1/2 mile off) by night, or keeping two-hour watches alternately through the night. You see I had plenty of time to write to you . . . In the early morning I strolled along my watch and watched an aeroplane high up, very faint in the dull light, heading for the German lines. [I] spent a quiet and pleasant day. In the line it was much harder work, very exciting at times and most of the time very tiring, but always fun, except when sad things happen. We were in a quiet part of the line, but even so there was a good deal of noise, chiefly from our trench mortars and theirs. You know these are small guns fired from just behind the trenches. They are very powerful and make a fearful row and break down trenches where they land . . . We came down yesterday to this place only about 1 1/2 miles from the firing line as general reserves. I don't quite know our next move. Perhaps up again. This place is a very small town or a very large village, sort of Royston touch.[36] Every other house is not there at all if you follow my meaning, and those that are have not got roofs or doors or walls or something else. A few months ago the Germans shelled this place heavily and have ruined the buildings. The people still live here and, to a great extent, nearly all are poor people. It is very funny to see them going along and living as if nothing was going on . . . The place is shelled from time to time but has not been for some time now. There are dugouts all over the place to rush into in case. Our Co[mpany] mess is in a house in a very poor part. It is about the only house in the street which has a roof and four walls to it, and even here there is not a pane of glass to be seen. My own billet is with two other fellows in a large house, rather forbidding looking. It is uninhabited except for one miner, a bachelor of whom we see little as he is early to work.

Well, this is all real fun. I enjoy it ever so, as indeed I do everything. I like France and the people too, not only for their novelty either. I think they are more friendly and less stiff than English people, which is a pleasant change. I love trying to talk to them, they are very decent. Next door there is a family, very poor and very dirty, but I don't think more so than English people; a little girl and two or three little boys . . . They have a nanny goat and billy goats and a little kid, opposite in a very dirty shed. We have conversations together, though we have a little trouble sometimes in making our meaning clear, though not very much considering . . .

Last night I slept on a mighty mattress by a window, as I have never slept in my life before, for in the line sleep is like a precious stone for its rarity. Getting up every other two hours to do a two hour watch spoils any bit you may get. The other night I did from eight in the morning till six thirty next morning, without a break. That was exceptional, but still you can see that it is tiring, and very nice to have a good lie sometimes.

One thing here (besides the people) is simply lovely, that is the flowers in the trenches. As you go up along the communication trench it is like nothing I have ever seen anywhere. I could really go into raptures over them. They grow on the top of the trenches and form a sort of arch bending over and meeting in the middle. These are what I have seen: cornflowers, poppies, daisies, wild mustard, buttercups, purple vetch, white and pink vetch, rest harrow, fumitory, clover, a sort of white or cream flower, half wallflower half stock, I don't know the name, and many others some of which I forget, and others which I don't know. In places you look along, and in front of you are banks of the bluest cornflowers in the world, and the reddest poppies in other places . . .

You have heard of the rats in the trenches, well unless you see them you can hardly imagine how many there are, nor how large. Walking along the trenches on a watch of two hours, you can see a hundred easily if you hadn't something else to look out for, and as it is, scores force themselves on your sight and, in the dugouts, on your person.

Now I will close for the moment, but hope to write again very shortly. Have received Homer, Dictionary, Wordsworth, Virgil, ear protectors, and a big parcel (the last about two hours ago), for all of which, and the many letters, very many thanks. It is very kind of you all to send me these things. Letters are very welcome here . . .

love to all,
Louis.

[Note included with letter dated 26 July 1916]
Last night after I had finished my letter I went from the mess back to my billet and opened my parcel by candlelight in my room.

What a wonderful parcel! You ought to have seen my delight as I unfolded pencils, chocolate, sweetmeats, books and so on, not to mention stacks of letters.

Well, to each one who sent me things, or wishes, in this parcel, I give my thanks many times repeated. I am now well off for literature; the chocolate, at the moment of writing, is not yet finished, although I and the fellow who is billeted with me did a certain amount of good work upon it last night, and before breakfast this morning. Also I woke up in the night and ate some. I sleep luxuriously now on the most wonderful mattress in the world, which I should think you could drop on to from a great height without injury, and with my great coat and waterproof sheet over me, I am in perfect comfort. This morning while dressing I saw a strange sight disappearing round the corner. A whole collection of people, old men, old women, young men, young women, little children, all dressed up in Sunday best, and strange wooden shoes, black hats and capes and all sorts. In the middle was a sort of stretcher with something on it covered up. There must have been about a score of people all together. Perhaps it was a funeral, but it disappeared before I could really see properly.

Love from Louis.

2nd Battalion
Royal Marines
B.E.F.
France
30th July 1916

Dear Mother and Dad,

Thank you very much for the letters I get from day to day; you can't send too many I don't think.

I am now up again in the trenches, after having a good rest in the town. I do not know how long we are here for or what we shall do next.

. . . You would enjoy watching the aeroplanes too, all day long they go to and fro over the lines, sometimes miles up, and sometimes low, and every now and then German or British anti-aircraft guns fire on some aeroplane. This looks very pretty . . . They fire sometimes 100 shots at one aeroplane, but I have never seen one hit yet. The aeroplanes themselves take comparatively little notice.

Then at night time you would like to watch the flares or Very's lights as they are called, which all night long mount slowly into the sky and sometimes half a dozen at once, as far as you can see, hang in the air lighting the country for half a mile around, and then slowly fall leaving a trail of bright smoke behind. They are very pretty, though often very inconvenient . . .

The other night I had supper in his dugout with a trench mortar officer. He had been two years at Cambridge when the war started . . . He had lost his ear protectors so I gave him mine. A trench mortar officer wants them, for these things make a fearful noise when you are close to them, but an infantry officer has no need of them. Although thank you very much for them. You see they came in useful . . .

With love from Louis.

2nd Battalion
Royal Marines
B.E.F.
France
2nd August 1916

Dear all,

We have just come down from the trenches again to the same little town for another rest. We were up quite a short time and things were very quiet.

The weather has been sweltering, even at night . . . and now I am in slacks again for the first time since you saw me last, and shall sleep in pyjamas tonight and not in clothes, which I have not done for three weeks; not that it is uncomfortable, but still pyjamas, I think, will be refreshing. We have got a new mess here this time, in quite a country little road with a field beside the house. My bedroom is over the mess, but the three other officers are billeted elsewhere. There is a bed in my room, and as I have already had a very all-embracing wash, I am really feeling like some young prince.

. . . Well, I like this very well. It is quite often exciting and nearly always funny; but I have not been in a bad place yet, so my experience is slight both in quantity and quality . . .

with love from Louis.

[Postcard]
8/8/16

Just a line at 5 a.m. to let you know we are up again. I am doing nicely. Heard Rugby beat Marlborough. Floreat Rugbeia! Now goodbye, love to all.

Louis M. Stokes.

2nd Battalion
Royal Marines
B.E.F.
France
13th August 1916

Dear Dad,

I must just write you a letter, to answer one or two things in your letters.

You say you are going to put down my name for Corpus. Thank you very much. There are, however, one or two things about that. What about the expense? Also you say that I can join the University directly the war is over. Well, it seems to me that when the war is over that King and country will still need the services of many of the forces for a certain time. Of course, I am not referring to a permanent commission, but I think there will probably be a good deal of 'dirty work' . . . It does not seem to me it would be fair to clear out as soon as all the fun was over, and leave the hard work to others . . .

You have asked about the tone of the soldiers. They are of course very rough and have no outward show, but they are to a man, I think, good fellows in the best sense . . . The very hardness and danger of their lives (the majority of this Battalion have been from England a twelvemonth and some nineteen months without leave, coming straight from Gallipoli where they landed first and left last) and the invariable cheerfulness which surprises us sometimes are the signs, rough and ready signs, of goodness in them. How often Lord French and Sir D. Haig have said, 'the men are beyond praise'. That phrase is well worn, but it is the only phrase . . .

You asked me if I read Homer or Virgil. Yes, I do, but I do not read much . . . for I find them too good usually. I like something light like the papers and the articles in them . . . Even so if I do read serious things then I read one of them or 'David Copperfield' or 'The Bible' or 'Prayer Book', which I must say I like . . .

Now goodbye, with love from
Louis.

2nd Battalion
Royal Marines
B.E.F.
France
Sunday 13th August 1916

Dear all,
Thank you very much for letters received since I last wrote . . . All of these were very interesting in common and different ways. But I must declare that what I like better than anything else since I have been here, indeed in any letter I have ever received there

has been nothing better, was the cutting of the Rugby-Marlboro' match giving me the score. . . .[37]

Well, well. We are down again in billets, a ripping place this time and only about 1 mile further than last time, but in a much nicer village . . . Now I have been sent to another place about 3/4 mile away to do five days bombing course and afterwards a gas course, I believe, so I shall miss the trenches for a day or two. I am pretty fed up, but I have got to go through these courses some time. I might as well get it over. I hate this loafing around on courses . . . I am very well and having lovely weather, but wish I wasn't doing this course.

Now goodbye and love to all,
Louis.

Purbright
Chislehurst
Kent
16th August 1916

Dear Stokes,

Many thanks for your letter and congratulations. I had the time of my life at Marlborough. The whole show was one colossal rag from beginning to end and you can hardly imagine how thrilling the match was. The match was a great triumph for riotous living. We drank, we smoked, we sat up till the early hours of the morning, while they were absolutely the reverse. We had a pretty rag in the train going there in spite of the fact that R.E. [Prior][38] and Payne-Smith[39] were accompanying us. However, we did not really get warmed up till later in the day. They had an absolutely priceless concert. Unpopular musicians were hissed, and eight beaks sang 'Simple Simon'. I have tried to choose eight beaks at Rugby, who would roughly correspond to the eight that sang, and I should think the following would suit: Steel, Lockhart, Sam B., Spitter, Hawker, Dickinson, G.F. Bradby, Whitelaw.[40] Can you imagine it? After this we wandered up and down High Street singing various songs, and caused much consternation amongst the inhabitants. Divers aged men put their heads out of their windows desiring to know what in the devil was happening. We gradually dropped off to bed, the last at about 4 a.m. At about 6 a.m. we were woken up by the College going home . . . At 11 a.m. the game started . . . It is an interesting point that those who got to bed before midnight averaged forty-eight in the first innings, while those who went to bed after midnight averaged eleven. On the close of play we had a glorious bathe in an open air tosh. Robinson,[41] who officially came as reporter to the 'Meteor', but in reality as Lockhart described, XI buffoon, and Lyon[42] gave an exhibition called the 'Drowning Man' . . . After this we had a dinner, followed by a sing song. The Marlborough XI were dull in extreme with three exceptions. Robinson therefore came to the conclusion things wanted livening up . . . [he] asked me if I could inform him where a gown and mortar board were to be obtained. I happened to have discovered one the night before, so I conducted him to it. In a few minutes Robinson appeared in his new garb looking a priceless bird. We proceeded to chase him all round the college grounds. Finally he was caught and a scrap ensued, the gown ripped in twain, and the mortar board received severe injuries . . . Highton[43] next morning collected the XI and said he was disgusted with our behaviour, and said we had so disgraced the name of the school that he was going away at once. (Cheers and prolonged laughter.) He took many exaggerated reports to Rugby, but as nothing has happened it matters little.

Things promised to be rather dull as Robinson and Lyon departed that evening, but the contrary proved to be the case. We ragged Canning horribly. There was a fire escape in the form of a ladder going up to his window. We climbed this and made weird tappings on the window and on the roof. Canning, who was trying to jaw three men with a view to becoming prefects, kept on saying, 'Hark at those jackdaws or rooks'. On retiring to the san more frivolity followed and at one o'clock the sister there entered in a dressing gown and informed us that the College boys did not make such a noise. Next day Sawyer[44], Kittermaster, and myself set out to get to camp. We started at 9.30 a.m., but failed to get very far. At the end of four hours we had got to Swindon, a distance of twelve miles. However, the delay was worth it as we suddenly saw a train enter with Robinson leaning out of the window with Bradby, who were also endeavouring to get to Fawsley [camp]. At length we proceeded. At every stop Robinson dashed off to get a cherry brandy. At Banbury we went to a kinema and nearly missed our connection . . . When we got to Rugby we found the last train had gone, so we decided to do the thing in style. We began by having dinner at the Silver Grill, and we intended to set off for Fawsley at 9.15 by motor. Robinson, of course, had lost his uniform which did not accelerate matters. We eventually got to camp at 11.30 after being delayed on the way by a puncture. Evers was awfully sick at our late arrival. In the middle of camp Robinson got a reply to his apology to Dr Penny whose gown he had torn. He was awfully sporting, saying he could quite understand the whole affair, and it was just the finale he wished his gown to meet with, as he could not bear to think of it slowly decaying in his study . . .

There were six terrific birchings last term . . . Darby[45] was awfully badly mashed up. The wretched little Inglis[46] . . . was also a victim . . . David made the poor wretch bleed . . . The *Rugby Opinion,* which was suppressed by David last term, appeared once more. The above suppression proved such an advertisement that it sold out in one hour . . .

Yours,
W.L.H. Pattisson.[47]

2nd Battalion
Royal Marines
B.E.F.
France
24th August 1916

Dear all,
    . . . Well, I am on a gas course of all horrible things on this earth, but I am glad to say it only lasts two and a half days, one of which is now over. I hate leaving the Battalion. I had to come down from the trenches for it, but not before I had had a nice little go there I am glad to say . . . I am billeted in rather a superior sort of house, that I think must have been a sort of country hotel at one time. . . . You don't have much to do with the people you are billeted with, except to say, 'Bonjour, Bonsoir', etc . . .

Love from Louis.

2nd Battalion
Royal Marines
B.E.F.
France
5th September 1916

Dear all,

There is nothing particular to tell you, except that I am as well as a blackberry and having good fun. Or as one of my platoon sergeants always starts his letters, 'My darling wife and little ones, here we are again all happy and bright'.

Last week it poured with rain and was very dirty weather for five to six days. The trenches were dreadfully muddy; up to the knees in places in water and sometimes for yards over the ankles in water or mud, and very slippery. It is really frightfully funny to walk solemnly along through a foot of muddy water . . .

The flowers are now dying and draggled, but running to seed, but in places are lovely still, especially chicory, which is very abundant round here, in light – almost Cambridge – blue . . .

Mother asks me if I want anything. Well, I should like you please to send me a toothbrush, as mine is almost worn out, and some Colgate's toothpaste as I have just come to the end of mine . . . I must say this about parcels, I don't think it's worthwhile your spending money on chocolates etc, which we can get out here fairly easily. The only thing to eat that I really think would be nice from time to time is a cake; because you cannot get them here and it is pleasing for all to see a cake on the table sometimes too. The things I need chiefly are matches, which are rather hard to get here, so if ever you send a parcel, if you just put two or three match boxes, a strongish sort of box if possible, in I should be very pleased . . .

Now love to all,
Louis.

2nd Battalion
Royal Marines
B.E.F.
France
12th Sept. 1916

Dear Margaret [Stokes]
. . . I have had occasion to read a good deal of Kipling's stories
and poems since I have been out here, because one of our officers
in this company is very keen indeed and has all the Kipling books.
. . . But I read very little. There is so much to do in one way
that although there are long periods of leisure, one is usually so
tired or hungry that eating, drinking and sleeping, and slow
contemplation of life, with reading of light things of interest such
as papers and looking again and again at things you are really fond
of like D[avid].C[opperfield]., Homer, Virgil and Lavengro etc.
are the occupations
But it is great fun. Sometimes of course it is sad enough, but
'things like that you must must be' . . . can you send me as soon
as possible:
1. 'The Coward' by E.F. Benson
2. 'Five Sonnets' by Rupert Brooke (or his works)
. . . I shall be very pleased if you can do this. I want to give
Dewar 'The Coward' to read. You would like Dewar. So would all
of you, he is topping.

Now goodbye,
with love from Louis.

2nd Battalion
Royal Marines
B.E.F.
France
12th Sept 1916

Dear all,
. . . I now write to say I am in the 'pink' and I hope all of you
are the same and enjoying yourselves as much as I am.
. . . The last week has been quite fine, and the trenches have
dried up . . . I am billeted in the kitchen of a cottage, at least it
has quite a large stove in it, and I am on the ground floor, so I
suppose it is the kitchen. The people are always very pleasant and

obliging wherever we have been stayed, though they have an inconvenient habit of going out for what they call a 'promenade', and locking the house up. One night on my bombing course I was constrained to climb in to my room, on the top storey, by means of a ladder I found.

With best love and thanks for all letters etcetera.

from Louis.

Headquarter School of Signalling
IVth Army Corps
B.E.F.
France
17th Sept 1916

Dear all,

Here I am on a month's signalling course, absolutely fed up. This is all I have to say at present for I am so enraged at the prospect of loafing about here for one solid month. I should not mind so much if the Battalion were not in the trenches, but as it is, it is simply rotten . . .

Will close now,
love from Louis.

Headquarter School of Signalling
IVth Army Corps
B.E.F.
France
25th September 1916

Dear all,

Tonight I have had a remarkable mail, consisting of one cake, in perfect condition, tooth brush and powder, matches, fruitcakes, etc . . . Also one huge and rich cake elaborately packed by a London firm called Gunter, which in the absence of any evidence to the contrary, I am going to assume comes from Daisy Mander . . . The cake, my dear mother, arrived just as it left you, I should think, in perfect condition, and a very good one indeed . . .

Now love to all,
from Louis.

165

Headquarter School of Signalling
IVth Army Corps
B.E.F.
France
26th Sept 1916

Dear Margaret,
 . . . I have not read many new books since I first read *David
Copperfield*. At Rugby I used to have that and Stevenson's *Across
the Plains* or *Memories and Portraits* always in my den, or practically
always, during my last two years.
 I would give anything to be at school again. Strange isn't it? . . .

Now I will knock off for a bit.
with love from Louis.

Headquarter School of Signalling
IVth Army Corps
B.E.F.
France
30th Sept 1916

Dear all,
 . . . I can well understand your excitement at seeing the airship
 . . . How well I remember the airship that, on another September
Sunday morning four years ago, hung in silence by the Roman
Catholic church at six o'clock in the morning; how we all from the
highest to the humblest arose and rushed forth from our beds and
gazed wildly on that Sabbath morning in years gone by ere ever the
Hun declared his hate of us and when babies slept safely in their
cradles. ('Shame!')
 . . . I am absolutely fed up with this signalling; it doesn't interest
me one bit. In fact, it bores me to the verge of tears, all about
cables and electricity and so on, that I don't understand and don't
want to . . .

love to all from
Louis.

2nd Royal Marines
B.E.F.
France
4th October 1916

Dear all,

I am back with my Battalion all right; at which you will guess I am pretty pleased, as I really had another fortnight to do at that dreadful course.

I am sorry that I cannot tell you what I am doing and where, but it is best I think to say absolutely nothing . . .[48]

Yesterday I came part of the way back from IVth Corps in a motor omnibus; it was funny sitting up in the front seat as though coursing along Regent Street or St Andrew's street. There were 'Pear's Soap' advertisements still on the backs of the seats. It was so worn that we had to get out and push it up hills! . . .

with love to all,
from Louis.

2nd Battalion
Royal Marines
B.E.F.
France
10th October 1916

Dear all,

. . . The men are very fine . . . I think their splendid cheerfulness redeems the shame which lies at someone's door, of this refusal of leave. We know too that they could have gone on leave and only a selfish Staff prevented it. The feeling out here is very bitter among some; chiefly perhaps among the officers who see the wrong done to the men but cannot prevent it. The Staff has done well often enough, but the times every day and all day when it might do more for the men (not the officers). Officers can more or less look after themselves. Men can be treated like dogs and at a safe distance.

. . . Still it's all fun here, and I am well enjoying everything and am glad to say I am absolutely 'in the pink' as regards health! If you could only see the stuff there's here one way and another! It shows what a war it is! In all parts of this country, it seems, hundred and hundreds of motor lorries, horse wagons, guns, ammunition, food, clothing, equipment. £5,000,000 a day is wanted, every penny of it . . .

<blockquote>With love to all, from Louis.</blockquote>

2nd Royal Marines
B.E.F.
France
14th October 1916

Dear all,

. . . Well, 'here we are again all merry and bright'. I have really nothing of news to tell you. I am very well indeed, I am thankful to say, and having the best of times. However, I must make a letter of it.

Now the winter is settling in. It is dark before six, and hardly light before that hour of the morning. There are more coldish days and less sun; the wind goes high and low and is scattering the leaves, though the trees are still green and heavy with leaves in places. Doubtless these phenomena are observed also in England.

Yesterday after tea I walked out of the village along the straight road with the lines of trees that always grow so here and turned off the road on to a great grass field on a rise, where the country stretched away, plough and pasture turning without hedge or ditch for miles to the wood in the far distance. I sat down by a haystack, a grey and dirty but drysmelling haystack. Two kestrels rushed up and with loud screams fluttered wildly in the air near by and departed ranging over the fields. As it got dark the flashes of the guns began to show in the distance; continual coming and going like summer lightning, and the bright Very lights ('star shells' the papers call them) rose slowly and hung like stars along the line; and from time to time a flash in the air like those in old picture books of the Matabele campaign or something showed where a shell was bursting; occasionally a string of green lights or green and red mixed floated into the distance, signals to artillery.

After some time I walked home past the everlasting streams of motor lorries that roar, and the horse wagons that battle past. I remember Mr Giffey telling me he had great arguments with brother officers who said they saw no romance in modern war; he said, 'there is romance in it'. How I agree with him! Dreadful it may be, and is too, but it is as romantic as it ever was.

I look back on the last page I have just written, and estimate its worth at about a farthing a line. However, I think you may have it for nothing . . .

Love to all,
Louis.

2nd Royal Marines
B.E.F.
France
17th October 1916

Dear all,
. . . Well, I find that I am an 'undergrad', which awes me not a little. I wonder when I shall lay aside the King's uniform and don the student's robes . . .

I am glad I did not accept the offer of sea service, which Capt Coode so pressed upon me; Clanchy is still at Forton Barracks and will be for a month or two yet, perhaps more, and then what a slow life he will have.

. . . This afternoon I was strafed by the adjutant on parade when drilling, because I was twiddling my stick round. I have got a renowned little stick now. It is a proper cane walking stick with a clawed handle, but it is broken and only about two foot long; a remarkable sight. Anyway, the adjutant said, 'You must keep your stick under your arm Mr Stokes, it looks very bad to twirl it'. Afterwards he told my company Captain I twiddled it like Charlie Chaplin . . .

Now I must say goodbye,
with love from Louis.

2nd Royal Marines
B.E.F.
France
20th October 1916

Dear all,
. . . I saw some marvellous flying today by some of our aero-planes; you never saw anything like it. They were just like swallows, turning in the air, swerving and diving and darting. They seemed gone crazy. I saw several tanks today over here, and

a German balloon (not a sausage observation balloon but an ordinary balloon) flying very high up in a northwesterly direction. It looked just like a ping pong ball in the bright sun. Suddenly it dropped a lot of literature; it must have been a couple of miles high. The papers looked rippling like silver fish in the blue sea . . . they floated and swayed and glittered . . . an aeroplane stood round trying to attack it, but I think it was too high . . .

Now goodbye. Love and best thanks to all,
from Louis.

2nd Royal Marines
B.E.F.
France
25th October 1916

Dear all,

Two months to Christmas! . . . Still I enjoy all this very much; there is a great deal of fun . . .

I read some Homer the other day; what different warfare theirs was! Fancy nowadays hardly ever seeing your enemy at all! All I have seen of the Boche has been dark forms at night against the blacker darkness of the sky; working on their parapet or patrolling, and those seldom. I have heard them talking away though; they are very noisy lads. When they see one of our 'toffee apples', as we call the medium sized trench mortar shell, coming towards their trench through the air, they blow loudly on French horns, and everyone (I suppose) rushes for cover. At least we do on this side when they send over the fell Minenwerfer or flying pig (which has kind of propelling wings to help it through the air); only we use whistles. The trench mortars are rather interesting because you can not only hear them coming but see them. They are tiny guns which are fired from support trenches and have a range of from 150–800 yards, and send sort of shells over into the hostile trenches. Both we and the Boche have several sorts. They go quite comparatively slowly through the air, often turning over and over and making a faint chuff-chuff-chuff sound . . .

with love and best wishes to one and all,
from Louis.

2nd Royal Marines
B.E.F.
France
30th October 1916

Dear all,

. . . For the last ten days we have been living on a great plateau
in tents and bivouacs; the men live in these last. I suppose there
are not enough tents. Bivouacs are waterproof(?) sheets made into
little sort of tents by being raised on sticks a few feet from the
ground. Seven men get into one and as there is a good squash they
are fairly warm I think, but I am afraid they are not very
comfortable as they can't help dragging a lot of mud in with them.
Washing and shaving is difficult especially as it has rained more or
less continuously for a week . . . The mud round here is just
wonderful, and nearly up to the knees in the trenches. It is a hard
time for the men now starting, as they get wet through without
anything to change into, day after day, while we have our valises
just now and so can change.

We are doing plenty of work, which is just as well; it has been
cold here lately. On Saturday (28th) Sir Douglas Haig came and
inspected this battalion late in the afternoon. He stopped and had
a short jaw with me. He asked me if the bivuoacs were waterproof.
I was sorry to have to say, 'No' (sir). He said 'H'm. H'm. Well
good luck', and shook hands with me. He looked different from
his pictures, much smaller, older and greyer, and tired. He had a
great train of generals behind him, they all jingled by with pennants
streaming. Quite an honourable sight.

My servant said he didn't want to see Sir Douglas Haig. He went
and picked apples instead. I told him he should honour the
Commander-in-Chief, and we held a long discussion upon military
things, during which the Battalion Sergeant Major entered my tent
on business, and affirmed that he honoured Sir Douglas Haig, and
declared he was the finest soldier in the army . . .

With best love to all,
from Louis.

2nd Royal Marines
B.E.F.
5th November 1916

Dear all,

It is about six o'clock in the evening and we have just come back a little way for a short rest after a month of hard work[49]. We have had a decent march today, not so very far, but far enough to try the men of this Battalion who are absolutely worn out, poor chaps. It is sad to see them; twenty months campaigning and no leave, barely enough food to live on, boots that are dropping off. Even so they are as cheerful as ever . . . but it's too much for them, and more and more go sick every day. We stopped halfway . . . on a great windy space among open fields and had dinner. The field kitchens drove up and stopped in front of each company and then there was hot soup with meat and peas in it for everyone, and hot tea with bread and jam. It was great fun and everyone seemed to enjoy it. Here I am in a ripping billet with my company captain, and a bed!

[continued on 6th November 1916]

Well I must tell you about my sleep last night. It was about the finest night's rest I have ever had. I slept in perfect comfort, and woke up – in perfect comfort – four or five times, just enough to feel 'how topping this is', and turn to sleep again. The ancient Romans of Nero's time . . . used to get their servants to wake them up at about one in the morning on purpose for them to think 'how ripping it is in bed' – then to sleep again. A good idea . . .

Love to all,
from Louis.

2nd Royal Marines
B.E.F.
France
11th November 1916

Dear all,

The night before last I came in at 12.30 having been on a long and muddy task since 3.00 p.m. I found a big parcel waiting for me with a cake, fruitcake, apples, sweets, nuts, lozenges and socks within. Thereupon I took off my puttees and boots, put on my great coat, all ready to go to bed, and sat down together with the other officer who had been with me. Nor did I rise from the festive board (there were the remains of supper on the table of honey, butter, cake, jam, bread) till 1.30 a.m. when 'replete with every modern convenience', I retired to my valise and woke up at 8.30 and devoured a hearty breakfast. What ho!

I write this so because I am getting tired of saying 'thank you' for the parcels and letters I receive. I am quite sure you cannot imagine the joy your letters and parcels give, so I just briefly draw the brutal picture and leave you to believe or not as you please, that I am most grateful . . .

I wish I could tell you what we are doing, but I can't. However, I am having great fun, as I hope you are.

Rotten letter this is. More follows.

Love from Louis.

NOTES TO PART THREE

1   J.Keegan, *The Face of Battle* (1978), p.224.
2   For a full account, see P. Simkins, *Kitchener's Army: The Raising of the New Armies, 1914–1916* (1988).
3   Keegan, *The Face of Battle*, p.224.
4   Public Record Office, WO 162/24.
5   Gen Sir H.E. Blumberg, *Britain's Sea Soldiers, A record of the Royal Marines during the War 1914–1919* (Devonport, 1927), p.468.
6   Ibid., p.463.
7   Ibid.
8   Ibid., p.468.
9   Ibid., p.464.
10   Ibid., p.312.
11   L. Macdonald, *Somme* (1983), p.321
12   Ibid., op cit.
13   A.P. Herbert, who was to become well-known as a writer, was an officer in the RND at this time. He wrote a poem about General Shute, which apparently became known throughout the RND and Army. The poem ended with the verse:

> For a shit may be shot at odd corners
> And paper supplied there to suit,
> But a shit would be shot without mourners
> If somebody shot that shit Shute.

(Quoted in Macdonald, *Somme*, p.322.)
14   Blumberg, *Britain's Sea Soldiers*, p.314.
15   Ibid.
16   Keegan, *The Face of Battle*, p.212.
17   See M. Middlebrook, *The First Day on the Somme* (1971); A.H. Farrar-Hockley, *The Somme*, (1964).
18   Macdonald, *Somme*, p.11.
19   Richard Henry Tawney (Whitelaw's 1894-9): served with 22nd Bn Manchester Regt; mentioned in despatches. Economist, lecturer and writer.

20 Quoted in T. Wilson, *The Myriad Faces of War* (1986), p.328.
21 Macdonald, *Somme*, p.305.
22 J. Buchan, *The Battle of the Somme: Second Phase* (n.d.), p.34.
23 Blumberg, *Britain's Sea Soldiers*, p.316.
24 Ibid.
25 For full details of the V Corps offensive in the Battle of the Ancre, see Capt W. Miles, *History of the Great War, Military Operations France and Belgium 1916* (1938), pp.485–497.
26 Blumberg, *Britain's Sea Soldiers*, p.319
27 Stokes to his parents, 11 November, 1916; see below p.173.
28 Extracts from the diary entries of 2nd Lieut John Austin Dewar, 2/RML1.
29 Rev F.P. David.
30 No one of this name appears in any records.
31 Leslie Kirkwood Phillips (Town 1911–12): served with Royal Marines; wounded.
32 Spencer Colin Browning (SH 1913–15): served with 87th Battery RFA; wounded.
33 In October, 1915, Lord Derby had introduced a scheme whereby men were invited to voluntarily 'attest' their willingness to serve. Married men who attested were assured that none of them would be called upon until all eligible bachelors had joined up.
34 Probably Arras. Between 14 July and 20 September, 1916, 1/RMLI and 2/RMLI relieved each other in frontline positions on the Angres II sub-sector of the Angres-Souchez sector of the line.
35 Heights of Notre Dame de Lorette.
36 Probably Hersin.
37 Rugby 268 (R.F. Wright 94) and 356 (F.R. Kittermaster 110, W.L.H. Pattisson 96); Marlborough 329 and 287 (L.A. Ashfield 129). Rugby won by 8 runs.
38 Robert Edward Prior, appointed as an assistant master in 1895; retired in 1926.
39 Rev William Henry Payne-Smith had temporarily rejoined the staff during the War, to help cover the shortages.
40 C.G. Steel, J.H.B. Lockhart, S. Barnard, Rev D.E. Shorto, C.E.M. Hawkesworth, B.B. Dickinson, G.F. Bradby and R. Whitelaw.
41 Alfred Esmond Robinson (SH 1912–16): served with 29th Battery RFA; awarded MC and Bar.
42 Captain of Rugby School XI v. Marlborough in 1916; Cambridge Cricket Blue 1921, 1922; see above p.76.
43 Highton was probably a master appointed on a temporary basis.
44 Charles Anthony Sawyer (G.F. Bradby's 1913–16): served with Oxford and Bucks Light Infantry.

45 John Henry Darby (G.F. Bradby's 1913–16): served with 28th Bn London Regt.
46 Alfred Walter Inglis (G.F. Bradby's 1913–17): served with 94th Brigade RFA, or his twin brother, Frederick Francis Inglis (G.F. Bradby's 1913–16): served with 2nd Bn Duke of Cornwall's Light Infantry.
47 William Laurence Hill Pattisson (Whitelaw's 1911–16): served with RNAS; awarded DSC; died of wounds on 17 March, 1918, at the German Military Hospital, Le Cateau.
48 On 4 October, 1916, 2/RMLI had travelled by train to Acheux, and then marched to Englebelmer, in preparation to join the Battle of the Somme. From 9–21 October 2/RMLI was based at Hedauville before returning to Englebelmer.
49 2/RMLI had moved back to Puchevillers.

EPILOGUE:

IN MEMORIAM

On 21 November, 1916, a small buff envelope was delivered to Rev Henry Stokes, marked 'Telegram, no charge for delivery'. Inside, in a scrawled carbon copy of the original, was the message, 'Deeply regret to inform you 2nd Lt Louis M Stokes RM killed in action 13th Nov Admiralty'. Two days later a further telegram arrived from Buckingham Palace. 'The King and Queen deeply regret the loss you and the Navy have sustained by the death of your son in the service of his country. Their majesties truly sympathize with you in your sorrow. Keeper of the Privy Purse.'

It is impossible to ascertain the exact circumstances of Louis' death. The Commanding Officer of 2/RMLI, Colonel A. Hutchison, described Louis being killed, 'whilst very gallantly leading his men in an attack on the German trenches.'[1] Captain A. Staughton, Louis' immediate superior, chose him to lead the first wave into action; he wrote, 'The last I saw of him was when I shook hands with him before he went into action.'[2] A further letter apologizes for not being able to provide much information: 'Stokes was last seen amongst a crowd of Scotch soldiers, the 7th Gordons, rushing forward to attack . . . he was picked up and buried by the Gordons.'[3]

Twenty-four officers from 2/RMLI took part in the attack on 13 November; fourteen were casualties. Five officers died, including Lieutenant L.J. Dewar, whose diary entry had asked for prayers prior to the attack; one officer later died of wounds and eight were wounded.[4] Louis' death, although a shattering blow to his family, was no more remarkable or courageous than hundreds of others on that day, or thousands of others throughout the War.

Letters of condolence to the Stokes family arrived from all quarters. Dr David wrote, 'I can enter into your sorrow because I loved your boy. I can never forget him, if only because he taught me.'[5] Roger Raven, a School House tutor, gave an address to the House, on 23 November 1916, about Louis. Raven spoke of how Louis 'loved every single enthusiastic moment of the short life he has now given up for us', and of Louis' 'originality and brilliance as a personality . . . his humour, thoughtfulness and lack of convention.'[6] A contemporary of Louis' at both St Faith's and School House wrote: 'Less than a year ago we had him with us, always cheerful and helping others to be so, and now he is gone. But he would not have had it otherwise. To take his chance with the rest was what he would want to do.'[7] C.W. Maule referred to Louis simply as a 'dear and noble boy'.

Such letters would have been written many times over by David and masters at Rugby. The total number of Rugbeians who served in the War was finally calculated at 3,299. Of those, 683 lost their lives (20.7 per cent) and 1,111 were wounded (33.7 per cent). Officers were more likely to lose their lives than those in the ranks, and most of the Rugbeians killed were commissioned (647 out of 683). However, their chances of death were still far greater than the average for an officer. Of all officers who served in the Army, 15.2 per cent were killed, and of other ranks, 12.8 per cent were killed.[8] The figures for the number of Old Rugbeians killed compares similarly with those of other major public schools: 1,157 Old Etonians were killed (the most of any public school) out of 5,660 who served (20.4 per cent); 749 Old Marlburians were killed out of 3,418 who served (22.0 per cent); 686 Carthusians were killed out of 3,000 who served (22.9 per cent).[9] It is difficult to explain this apparent disparity between the chances of death for a public schoolboy, compared to that of others who served. It may have been that more public schoolboys joined the Services in the early months of the War and the chances of death were greater.[10] It may have been that the public-school ethos of bravery and leadership meant more young officers were killed setting an example of selflessness and good conduct to their men. It may have been that more joined the Infantry, and more fought in the dangerous theatres of the War. Whatever the reason, there is no doubt that Rugby, like most public schools, lost a generation of pupils.[11]

Ninety-six boys, including Louis, entered Rugby in September, 1911. Of those, eighty-nine served in the Armed Forces, three in the French Red Cross, one in the British Red Cross, one in the American Ambulance Field Service, and two were in the protected occupations of doctor and teacher. Twenty-one of Louis' entry were killed in action, twenty-six were wounded and one was taken Prisoner of War. Eleven were awarded the Military Cross and five the Croix de Guerre.

The sacrifice of Rugbeians was far-ranging.[12] Of the 647 officers who died, there were 2 Lieutenant-Generals, 1 Major General, 1 Brigadier-General, 4 Colonels, 26 Lieutenant-Colonels, 57 Majors, 191 Captains, 181 Lieutenants, 165 Second Lieutenants, 3 Cadet Officers, 7 Chaplains, and 9 others. Of the other ranks, 2 Sergeants, 3 Corporals, 8 Lance Corporals and 23 Privates died. The average age of those who died was twenty-nine years, with the youngest being eighteeen and the oldest sixty-eight. Apart from Louis, fifty-nine other Old Rugbeians died aged nineteeen. Two old Rugbeian Members of Parliament died, four Heads of School and twenty-three Heads of Houses (including six Heads of School House). A total of 3,159 Honours were awarded to Old Rugbeians ranging from four VCs[13] to four Orders of the Furious Tiger (China). In addition, 497 MCs were awarded (plus forty-four Bars to MC, and three Second Bars), 216 DSOs and 342 foreign decorations; 1,621 men were mentioned in despatches. Old Rugbeians were killed in every one of the fifty-two months of the War, twelve were killed on the first day of the Battle of the Somme, and a further six on 2 July, 1916.

Four Rugbeian families suffered the tragedy of having three sons die in the War. The Buckley Roderick family from Carmarthenshire lost their youngest son Allan Whitlock Nicholl Buckley Roderick (G.F. Bradby's 1910–12) 4th Bn Welsh Regiment, on 9 August, 1915, in Gallipoli, aged nineteen. Their eldest son, Captain Hume Buckley Roderick (Collins' 1901–6) Welsh Guards, was killed at Gouzeaucourt on 1 December, 1917, aged thirty. He had married a year earlier, and his wife's father, Lieutenant Colonel R. Garnons Williams had been killed at Loos on 27 September, 1915. Captain Hume Buckley Roderick's daughter was born seven months after his death in June, 1918. The final tragedy occurred on 21 August, 1918, when the third brother, Lieutenant John Victor Tweed Buckley Roderick (G.F. Bradby's 1911–13) lst Bn Coldstream Guards, was killed at Moyenneville on 21 August, 1918, aged twenty-one.

Two Old Rugbeian fathers and sons also died in the War. One of the fathers was the famous hunter, explorer and author Frederick Courteney Selous (J.M. Wilson's 1866–8). He joined the Royal Fusiliers in February, 1915, served in East Africa and was killed on 4 January, 1917, aged sixty-five. His son, Frederick Hatherley Bruce Selous (SH 1912–15), Royal West Surrey Regt and RFC, was shot down and killed over the German lines above the Menin Road on the first anniversary of his father's death, aged nineteen. Lieutenant Francis John Hadden (Elsee's 1875–9) 42nd Sqn Remount Service, died in Cairo on 5 May, 1916, aged fifty-four. His son, Lieutenant Arthur Hadden (Collins' 1906–8) Indian Army, was killed in Mesopotamia on 8 March, 1916, aged twenty-three.

The 6th Bn Manchester Regiment provides another telling example of Rugbeian service. In the attack on the Turkish trenches at Achi Baba, on the Gallipoli Peninsula, in early June, 1915, ten Old Rugbeian officers were involved from this one Regiment. Four were killed and, of the remaining six, two were killed later in the War and four were wounded. In addition to those of the 6th Bn Manchester Regiment, a further five other Old Rugbeians also died in the assault on Achi Baba between 4–6 June, 1915.

The understandable move to commemorate the dead began almost immediately after the start of the War. The first Memorial Service to those Old Rugbeians who had died was held on 1 November, 1914, in the school Chapel. A War Register of the school was begun soon after the declaration of War, and the first edition was issued in November, 1914, listing 1,100 serving Old Rugbeians and details of the thirty-eight killed and forty-six wounded. Second and third editions of the Register were published, before the Government prohibited further publication of such Registers. A fourth edition was published in February, 1919, and a fifth and definitive edition in 1921.[14] Seven volumes of *Memorials of Rugbeians who fell in the Great War* were also published between 1915 and 1923, with a portrait and biography of all those who died. Each volume is dedicated 'To Rugbeians of all generations who in it may learn how much they owe to the brave men who at the call of duty fought for the honour of their country and following the great example willingly laid down their lives for others'.

On 4 April, 1917, at a meeting in Drapers' Hall, London, a Memorial Fund was started with the objectives of erecting a permanent memorial in Rugby, and also providing for the education at Rugby of the sons of those who died in the War. On 19 June, 1920, a Lantern Cross designed by Sir Charles Nicholson[15] was unveiled and now stands outside the school's Macready Theatre. A Memorial Chapel also designed by Nicholson, was built on the Close, connecting with the main school Chapel. It is in the shape of a Greek Cross with a five-light window in each arm, and the names of 686 Old Rugbeians inscribed on the walls of the transepts. The Memorial Chapel dedication was performed on 8 July, 1922, by two former headmasters: Dr A. David, Bishop of St Edmundsbury and Ipswich; and Dr H.A. James, President of St John's College, Oxford. Dr W. Temple, Old Rugbeian, Bishop of Manchester, gave the address. In the Memorial Chapel is an oak lectern, surmounted by a bronze figure of an OTC cadet in memory of Lieutenant W. Littleboy.[16] The lectern houses the seven volumes of *Memorials of Rugbeians who fell in the Great War*.

Louis was buried in Mailly Wood Cemetery, five and a half miles north of Albert. He is also commemorated on the memorials in St Faith's Preparatory School, Corpus Christi College, Rugby School Memorial Chapel and Little Wilbraham Parish Church. Such memorials gave physical manifestation to the grief of a nation; Louis' most important memorial today is his letters.

NOTES TO EPILOGUE

1   Col A. Hutchison to Rev H. Stokes, 14 December. 1916
2   Capt A. Staughton to Rev H. Stokes, 12 December, 1916. Staughton wrote this letter from a bed in the 20th General Hospital, France, and later died from wounds sustained on 13 November 1916.
3   F. Powell to Sgt W. Meatyard, 24 December, 1916.
4   Blumberg, *Britain's Sea Soldiers*, p.318.
5   Dr A. David to Rev H. Stokes, 25 November, 1916.
6   R. Raven to Rev H. Stokes, 24 November, 1916.
7   M. Bateson to Rev H. Stokes, 27 November, 1916.
8   General Annual Report of the British Army 1917–1919, PP 1921, XX, Cmd 1193.
9   See C.F. Kernot, *British Public Schools War Memorials* (1927).
10 Between 10 October, 1914, and 30 September, 1915, 14.2 per cent of officers in the Army were killed; between 1 October, 1917, and 30 September, 1918, 6.9 per cent of officers were killed.
11 See J.M. Winter, 'Britain's "Lost Generation" of the First World War', *Population Studies*, XXXI (1977), pp.449–66.
12 The authors are indebted to R. David R. Ray for the statistical information contained in this paragraph.
13 Lieutenant Frank Alexander de Pass, see above p.127 note 52; Captain Christopher Bushell (SH 1901–6); Lieutenant Geoffrey St George Shillington Cather (Wilson's 1905–8); Lieutenant Robert Vaughan Gorle (Dickinson's 1910–11).
14 *Rugby School War Register, Containing the Names and Services of Rugbeians in the Great War of 1914–1918* (Rugby, 1921).
15 Charles Archibald Nicholson (SH 1881–6).
16 Wilfrid Evelyn Littleboy (SH 1909–14): served with 16th Bn Royal Warwickshire Regt; killed near Gheluvelt on 9 October 1917.

INDEX

INDEX OF NAMES AND PLACES

Lyon, Malcolm Douglas, 42, 52, 65, 76, 161, 176
Lyon, Percy Hugh Beverley, 37, 75
Lyttelton, Edward, 127

MacLean, Walter Alexander, 45, 76
Mailly Wood Cemetry, 183
Mander, C. B., 6
Mander, Charles Tertius, 48, 76
Mander, Daisy, 165
Mander, J. H., 7
Margate, 6
Marlborough College, 20, 158, 160–1
Matthews, Colonel, 143
Maule, C. W., 180
Mayne, Cyril, 35, 47, 50, 75
Meerholz, Mr, 109–10
Mouchy Bretton, 136

Newport, 146
Nicholls, Sir John, 143
Nicholson, Sir Charles Archibald, 183, 184
Notre Dame de Lorette, 135, 175
Notting Hill, 60, 75, 112
Nuthall, George Robert Falkiner Hans, 40, 75
Nuthall, Winfred Lawrence Falkiner, 40, 75

Odgers, Francis William, 98, 104, 126
Oratory School, The, 115
Oundle School, 122
Oxford, University of, 17

Paine, Rev., 61, 77
Paris, General A., 135
Pattisson, William Laurence Hill, 162, 175, 176
Payne-Smith, Rev. William, 86, 160, 175
Peile, Canon, 36
Penny, Dr, 162
Percival, Arthur Jex-Blake, 97, 126, 128
Phillips, Leslie Kirkwood, 145, 175
Pickles, J. D., 5
Plomer, William, 85, 87
Podmore, Hubert, 22, 23, 49, 74, 126
Pollen, A. H., 86, 114, 128
Porchester, Lord; Henry George Alfred Marius Victor Francis Herbert, 90–1, 95, 101, 126
Portsmouth, 135, 140, 142, 144, 146, 148, 149

Poulton, see Poulton-Palmer
Poulton-Palmer, Ronald William, 21, 63, 73, 109, 114
Powell, Kenneth, 63, 77
Pozières, 137
Prior, Robert Edward, 160, 175
Puchevillers, 176

Queen's College, Oxford, 25

Raven, Roger Abbot, 18, 22, 62, 64, 73, 104, 105, 145, 180
Raymond, Ernest, 82
Read, Brian Henderson, 45, 76
Robinson, Trevor Felix David, 34, 75
Rugby (town of), 46, 109–10
Rugby School, *passim*

St Faith's Prep. School, Cambridge, 7, 33, 62, 183
St Hill, Edward Ashton, 63, 77
St Paul's, Cambridge, 6
St Peter's, Wolverhampton, 6
St Pierre Divion, 138
Salisbury Plain, 84
Samson, Oswald Massey, 126
Sandhurst, 17, 82
Sawyer, Charles Anthony, 161, 175
Selous, Frederick Courteney, 181–2
Selous, Frederick Hatherley Bruce, 42, 43, 47, 52, 76, 182
Shaw, George Bernard, 24
Sheppard, Rev., 60
Sherriff, R. C., 133
Shorto, Rev. D. E., 77
Shrewsbury School, 102, 119
Shute, General C., 135, 174
Simey, Dr Athelstane Iliff, 44, 76
Simpson, James Herbert, 18, 22, 29, 30, 72
Slough, Orphan School, 6
Somme, the, 3, 136–7
Spens, Thomas Patrick, 40, 41, 75
Stanford, Henry Morrant, 115, 128
Staughton, Capt A., 179, 184
Steel, Anthony Bedford, 126–7
Steel, Charles Godfroy, 66, 77
Steel, Edwin Bedford, 99, 126
Stokes, Amy, 5, 7
Stokes, Rev. Henry Paine, 5, 6–7
Stokes, Rev. John, 6
Stokes, Uncle Louis, 6, 11
Stokes, Mary, née Kinton, 6
Stokes, Sophie Emmeline, née Mander, 5